D1558332

783

GLOBAL ORGANIZATIONS

The Association of Southeast Asian Nations

GLOBAL ORGANIZATIONS

The African Union

The Arab League

The Association of Southeast Asian Nations

The Caribbean Community

The European Union

The International Atomic Energy Agency

The Organization of American States

The Organization of Petroleum
Exporting Countries

The United Nations

The United Nations Children's Fund

The World Bank and
the International Monetary Fund

The World Health Organization

The World Trade Organization

GLOBAL ORGANIZATIONS

The Association of Southeast Asian Nations

Gerald W. Fry

Series Editor
Peggy Kahn
University of Michigan–Flint

CHELSEA HOUSE
PUBLISHERS

An imprint of Infobase Publishing

The Association of Southeast Asian Nations
Copyright © 2008 by Infobase Publishing

Chelsea House
An imprint of Infobase Publishing
132 West 31st Street
New York NY 10001

Library of Congress Cataloging-in-Publication Data
Fry, Gerald W. (Gerald Walton), 1942-
The Association of Southeast Asian Nations/by Gerald W. Fry.
  p. cm.—(Global organizations)
Includes bibliographical references and index.
ISBN 978-0-7910-9609-3 (hardcover)
1. ASEAN. I. Title. II. Series.

DS520.F79 2008
341.24'73—dc22   2008010497

Series design by Erik Lindstrom
Cover design by Ben Peterson

Printed in the United States of America

Bang KT 10 9 8 7 6 5 4 3 2 1

This book is printed on acid-free paper.

All links and Web addresses were checked and verified to be correct at the time of publication. Because of the dynamic nature of the Web, some addresses and links may have changed since publication and may no longer be valid.

CONTENTS

INTRODUCTION

Two Young Women, the Problem of Burma, and ASEAN

SAMTHIP IS 19 YEARS OLD AND IS A MEMBER OF THE SHAN ethnic group. Until fairly recently, her family lived in the northeastern Shan state of Myanmar (formerly Burma before 1989), a region of hills, mountains, and forests. Samthip and her mother, Jankham, began to hear stories of Burmese soldiers storming into Shan villages and brutally raping Shan women. They feared for their lives. They struggled to earn a living, because Myanmar is poor and offers limited job opportunities. About five years ago, in the middle of the night, Samthip, her mother, and her little brother, Sai, escaped by boat down a river that flows into Thailand. They now live in Mae Hong Sorn, in a remote northwestern part of Thailand. Samthip's father, Santhithammo, whose name means "the peaceful one," is a Buddhist monk who remains in Myanmar. Samthip and her family are only a few of an estimated 250,000 people who have fled violence and repression in Myanmar and now live in Thailand.

In September 2007, while living in Mae Hong Sorn in northwestern Thailand, Samthip and her family learned about new protests in Myanmar. Monks and others had been killed or injured during peaceful protests. The demonstrations erupted when the government increased the prices of oil and gas. The very difficult economic conditions and continuing harsh military rule also contributed to the protests. Although her father was not politically active, Samthip worried about him.

Samthip has tremendous admiration for Burmese who protest peacefully, especially for Aung San Suu Kyi, the leader of the political opposition group the National League for Democracy and winner of the Nobel Peace Prize in 1991. A Buddhist, Aung San Suu Kyi has been recognized for her nonviolent resistance against the Burmese military dictatorship. In 1990 the political party she led easily won an election, but military rulers confined her to her house rather than allowing her to become the country's leader. Samthip proudly displays pictures of Aung San Suu Kyi and the king of Thailand in her house in Thailand. She and her mother still revere the old Burmese kings who ruled before Great Britain made Burma their colony.

Since Samthip, her mom, and her brother are considered temporary residents of Thailand, they do not have official Thai citizen identity cards. Their temporary-resident status greatly limits what they can do. Samthip's movement is limited to several provinces near Myanmar; she cannot travel to the capital city of Bangkok or to south or northeast Thailand. Having an alien card also limits her opportunities to attend school or to work. On her own she is trying to improve her English by reading George Orwell's *Burmese Days*, a book based on his experiences working in Burma as an officer in the Indian Imperial Police in the 1920s.

Aung San Suu Kyi (above) won the 1991 Nobel Peace Prize for her attempts to bring democracy to Myanmar. Her struggle against the military junta in Myanmar has increased pressure on ASEAN to balance the needs of the region against the demands of the international community.

Although Samthip and her family are regarded as people displaced by political repression and violence in Myanmar, they do not have formal refugee status, so they cannot move to other countries such as the United States or Canada. On the other hand, many Karens, another ethnic community suffering in Myanmar, have attained refugee status, and there is a growing community of such individuals in the Twin Cities in Minnesota.

Daw Khin Khin has a very different story to tell. She is ethnically Burman. Seeing signs of trouble, her father, a Burmese ambassador, sent his daughter to study in the United States. Given the bad economic and political situation in Burma after the military takeover in 1962, Daw Khin Kin decided to stay in the United States. She has taught English to students from abroad who attend universities in the United States. She also has been politically active as part of the "Free Burma" movement, fighting for the restoration of democracy in her native country. Like Samthip, Daw Khin Khin has great admiration for Aung San Suu Kyi because of her nonviolent commitment to freedom. Daw Khin Khin once met Aung San Suu Kyi's son, Alex, at a reception in Washington, D.C.

Daw Khin Khin always calls her homeland Burma, never Myanmar, which is the name that was given to the country by the military government in 1989. This name change from Burma to Myanmar was recognized by the United Nations (UN), the Association of Southeast Asian Nations (ASEAN), and several Asian nations. However, it was not recognized by many Western governments, which continue to use Burma. The European Union uses Burma/Myanmar as an alternative.

These two different young women, Daw Khin Khin and Samthip, have been caught in the history of the country of their birth. Myanmar, a poor country with a military dictatorship, has strong opposition leaders and many gentle monks who remain guided by principles of democracy and freedom. Myanmar is a member of an organization of countries in the region, ASEAN. Founded in 1967, ASEAN is an organization of independent countries in the geographic region of Southeast Asia. Its objectives have been to strengthen the region's control over its own affairs, to create peace and stability among countries, and to expand trade and increase economic prosperity among its member countries.

For many years ASEAN, other organizations, and many political leaders have been trying to change the difficult situation in Burma, but ASEAN's work has been limited. In 1997 it invited Myanmar to become a member, despite its bad human rights record and repressive military regime, because it felt that the best strategy for changing Myanmar was to *engage* it, not to isolate it. ASEAN strongly criticized the Burmese military government for its violent suppression of human rights' demonstrations in 2007 but could not stop the killings of more than 45 people and about 2,000 arrests. ASEAN refused to meet with a special UN representative in November 2007 to discuss further measures against the Burmese government.

ASEAN was created to help Southeast Asian countries determine their own future and to create policies without outside interference and pressure by its former colonizers, the United States, or by strong regional powers. Thus, the organization has been reluctant to tell individual governments what to do. Nondemocratic ASEAN countries such as Vietnam and Laos tend to be more sympathetic to the Burmese government, or Myanmar regime, since they do not want any external interference with their own one-party political systems. To show its disapproval, ASEAN simply could reject Myanmar as a member. Some countries, such as Thailand, do not want to break relations with Myanmar because they have important joint economic projects. The Thai government relies on Burma for timber and natural gas since it banned logging years ago to help preserve its remaining forests.

If ASEAN were to show its teeth, it could do several things to influence political change in Myanmar. It could threaten to kick Myanmar out of ASEAN if it did not change its policies. It could call for a complete economic and tourist boycott of Myanmar. (A boycott, though, would negatively affect the economy of Burma's neighbor, Thailand, which depends on Myanmar's resources.) ASEAN could work closely with Myanmar's closest and most powerful neighbors—China, India, and Japan—which provide vital aid to the Burmese. ASEAN could try to convince the world community to boycott Myanmar totally, as it did successfully for Cambodia in earlier decades. Finally, it could try to lobby the world to boycott the 2008 Olympics in Beijing unless the Chinese place pressure on Burma to relax their repressive rule.

But it does not seem likely that ASEAN will take any of these roads. Instead, it will concentrate on economic and social progress within ASEAN countries rather than on safeguarding human rights or Western-style democracy. For example, a new initiative to improve the conditions and opportunities for migrant workers—workers who travel between the countries of the region because of violence or lack of economic opportunity at home, such as Samthip and her family—would help, even if Myanmar, their home, does not become a safer, more democratic, and more prosperous country.

Southeast Asia and ASEAN

"Today, ASEAN is not only a well-functioning, indispensable reality in the region. It is a real force to be reckoned with far beyond the region. It is also a trusted partner of the United Nations in the field of development. I hope that in the field of peace and security, too, we will see the beginnings of closer cooperation between ASEAN and the United Nations."[1]

—Kofi Annan, secretary-general of the United Nations (1997–2006), February 16, 2000

ON AUGUST 8, 1967, IN THE DEPARTMENT OF FOREIGN AFFAIRS in Bangkok, Thailand, foreign ministers of five countries— Indonesia, Malaysia, the Philippines, Singapore, and Thailand— signed the agreement known as the ASEAN Declaration or

Bangkok Declaration, which created ASEAN. These five foreign ministers, all high-level government officials in charge of their countries' policies, are considered ASEAN's founding fathers.

Two years before the establishment of ASEAN, Southeast Asian nations were going through turbulent times. ASEAN was created as an initiative to avoid outside involvement, violent conflict, and division in the region.

WHERE IS SOUTHEAST ASIA?

All ASEAN members are in the geographic area referred to as Southeast Asia. Naval doctor Benajah Ticknor first used the term in his journals and photographs of the region in the early nineteenth century.[2] Researchers and diplomats came to define Southeast Asia as Burma (renamed Myanmar in 1989), Cambodia (formerly Kampuchea), Indonesia, Laos, Malaya (later to become Malaysia in 1963), the Philippines, Singapore, Thailand (earlier Siam), and Vietnam. Later, when Brunei (in 1984) and East Timor (in 2002) became independent countries, they were categorized as being part of Southeast Asia. East Timor (Democratic Republic of Timor-Leste) is a new nation of the region but not yet a member of ASEAN.

The 11 countries in Southeast Asia occupy the lands, islands, and peninsulas between India and China. Southeast Asia usually is divided into two main geographic areas. The first is the peninsular or mainland region including Myanmar, Cambodia, Laos, Thailand, and Vietnam. The second is the insular or island region, including Brunei, East Timor, Indonesia, the Philippines, and Singapore. Malaysia includes part of a mainland area and part of the island of Borneo. The island portion of Southeast Asia has approximately 25,000 different islands. Two of the world's largest islands, New Guinea and Borneo, are there. Indonesia comprises over 17,000 islands and the Philippines, over 7,000.

The region as a whole is about the size of Europe, but much of it is ocean. The population is more than 550 million people. The world's fourth-largest country, with nearly 250 million

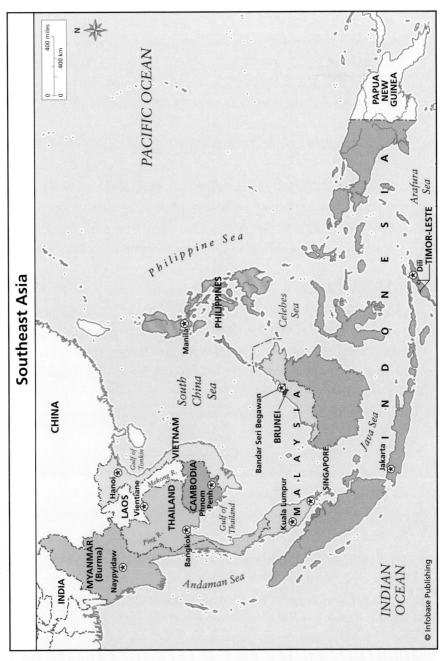

The vast area of Southeast Asia includes countries with different climates, cultures, and religions. While past conflicts created tense situations between some countries, ASEAN is working to maintain a level of security and peace in the region.

people, Indonesia dominates the region in population. Tiny Brunei has fewer than half a million people. Singapore has a population of a little over 4 million, and Laos has a little over 6 million. The large city of Bangkok in Thailand has roughly the same population as the three ASEAN countries of Laos, Singapore, and Brunei combined.

With the exception of landlocked Laos, all the countries in Southeast Asia have either Indian and/or Pacific Ocean coasts. Water is important, not simply in the sense that nearly all these countries have ocean coasts but also because rivers are extremely significant. These rivers are a valuable source of water and protein and provide vital transportation links for sending rice, for example, to major ocean ports. The mighty and majestic Mekong River is a prominent part of the physical and cultural landscape of Cambodia, Laos, Thailand, and Vietnam. The Mekong has giant catfish and freshwater dolphins. The Salween River runs from Tibet through Myanmar to Thailand. Areas along the Salween River have a vast variety of nature and wildlife.

Major mountain ranges are present in the northern parts of mainland Southeast Asia, and it even occasionally snows in the mountainous regions of northwest Vietnam. The entire area, except for high mountainous regions, has a warm tropical climate year-round. During monsoon season, heavy rains pour down when winds blow in from the Indian Ocean and the Arabian Sea.

Nearly all the world's great religions and philosophies— Islam, Buddhism, Confucianism, Christianity, Taoism, Hinduism, and animism (belief in and worship of spirits that inhabit natural bodies such as trees, forests, and mountains)—are represented in the region. Muslim traders probably brought Islam to Indonesia as early as the 1200s, and by the late 1600s Islam had become an important part of people's lives there. Indonesia has the world's largest Muslim population at 195.2 million, representing 12.5 percent of all Muslims in the world. In fact, 15 percent of the world's Muslims live in Southeast Asia.

COLONIALISM AND WARS FOR INDEPENDENCE

Three ASEAN countries (Vietnam, Laos, and Cambodia) are former French colonies; four (Brunei, Burma, Malaysia, and Singapore) are former British colonies or protectorates; Indonesia is a former Dutch colony; and the Philippines once was controlled by the Spanish and later by the United States. East Timor, most likely the next member of ASEAN, used to be ruled by Portugal. Only Thailand—through a combination of astute diplomacy and British and French rivalry for influence in the region—was able to avoid the European colonial control that dominated the area from about 1500 to 1946.

The peoples of Southeast Asia suffered severely under colonial rule. European imperial powers ran their colonies to extract resources and to benefit themselves rather than to improve the livelihoods of local peoples. Europeans thought themselves to be superior in intelligence, morality, and worth. Colonial rule did not prepare the Southeast Asian countries well for democracy, and a good education was generally provided only for a small elite population.

In what was then known as the East Indies (the lands of South Asia and Southeast Asia), the Dutch East India Company forced Indonesians to grow coffee and tea for Holland instead of rice, the staple needed by the people. This led to poverty and hunger. Similar abuses occurred in other parts of Southeast Asia. In Indochina (the French colony of Vietnam, Laos, and Cambodia), the French encouraged the Vietnamese to smoke opium and drink liquor so as to be able to collect taxes on those products. Anyone who tried to fight against French rule was harshly punished. In addition, in the Indo-Chinese colonies, the French looked down on the local languages, and they provided French-oriented education in the French language to elites cooperating with the French.

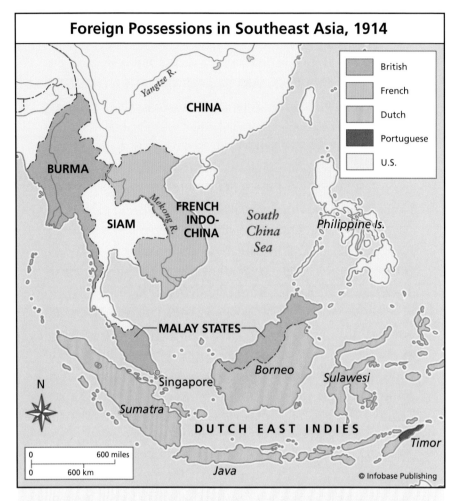

Foreign Possessions in Southeast Asia, 1914

Legend:
- British
- French
- Dutch
- Portuguese
- U.S.

CHINA

Yangtze R.

BURMA

SIAM

Mekong R.

FRENCH INDO-CHINA

South China Sea

Philippine Is.

MALAY STATES

Singapore

Borneo

Sulawesi

N

Sumatra

DUTCH EAST INDIES

Timor

Java

0   600 miles
0   600 km

© Infobase Publishing

Like their African counterparts, many member nations in ASEAN suffered under colonialism. After decades of European and American interference, some of these countries are becoming more developed and affluent while others, like Myanmar, continue to struggle.

The Philippines became a colony of Spain in the 1500s. Although the Spanish founded new towns; introduced new crops and livestock; and established schools, hospitals, and universities; the people of the Philippines yearned for independence. The Philippine Revolution against Spain (1896–1898), led by Emilio Aguinaldo, established the first Philippine republic. However, the Treaty of Paris, at the end of the Spanish-American War, transferred control of the Philippines to the United States. In response, the Philippine government declared war on the United States in 1899. During the Philippine-American War, there were massive Filipino casualties, and Emilio Aguinaldo was captured. Declaring victory in 1905, the United States took control of the Philippines. The United States granted the Philippines partial autonomy (commonwealth status) in 1935, with full independence planned for 1946. The Japanese occupied the islands during World War II.

In Malaysia, colonialism resulted in the migration of Chinese and Indian labor to work on rubber plantations and in the tin mines. Subsequently, the country ended up with large populations of both Malays and Chinese. There was serious racial tension, particularly in the 1960s, when the Penang race riots occurred.

World War II had a great impact on the region, with many battles fought there. During the war, Southeast Asia was strategic as a source of raw materials, such as rubber and tin, for the Japanese war machine, since Japan itself had few natural resources. Japanese strength in initially defeating Westerners in battle and supporting independence movements encouraged the Southeast Asian nations to fight for self-government.

The end of World War II was followed by the start of the Cold War between the Communist Soviet Union and the democratic and capitalist United States. With the North Korean invasion of South Korea on June 25, 1950, the Cold War became hot. Both the Soviet Union and China supported Communist movements in numerous Southeast Asian countries such as South Vietnam, Laos, Cambodia, the Philippines, Malaya, Thailand, and Indonesia. The United States felt extremely threatened by the growing geographic spread of Communism in Asia.

Due to the Cold War and the rise in popularity of the French Communist Party in France, the United States supported France in its war against Vietnamese independence. France was not successful in keeping control of its colony. In a peace treaty called the Geneva Accords, signed in 1954, Vietnam, then free of French control, was divided into the Communist North and the Western-backed South. In an effort to prevent the spread of Communism beyond North Vietnam, the South Vietnamese army, backed by the United States, went to war with Vietnamese Communist rebels. The Vietnam War, also referred to by many people as the U.S. War in Vietnam, was fought from 1959 to April 30, 1975. The U.S. government's policy rested on the belief that the South Vietnamese army could defeat the guerrillas on their own, but the quality of the South Vietnamese army was impaired by poor leadership, corruption, and governmental incompetence. In March 1965, U.S. troops were dispatched to South Vietnam. Despite a huge commitment of money and troops, the U.S. effort, like the French one before it, failed. Cambodia, South Vietnam, and Laos all became Communist countries in 1975 with the military victories of revolution-ary forces. Despite the success of Communism in these three countries, Communist movements failed in the Philippines, Malaysia, Indonesia, Burma, Singapore, and Thailand.

With the end of the Vietnam War, the eventual end of the Cold War, and the collapse of the Soviet Union in 1991, Southeast Asia again became strategic as a huge economic market and a major supplier of natural resources. The region has a current total population of more than 550 million people, roughly half the population of China, making it a huge and rap-idly growing market. The total nominal GDP—gross domestic product, the value of goods and services produced each year—of the region is $799 billion, roughly half that of China. In terms of international trade, the region is even more significant, with its total trade (imports and exports) roughly equal to that of China, which is an emerging economic giant in the world economy. Exports and international investment in the area have led to growth in the economies and rising standards of living for many in the region. On the other hand, large global companies have gone to Southeast Asia to find sources of cheap labor and raw materials, tourism has led to some women using their bodies to make money from visitors, and changes in economies have created environmental problems.

POLITICS IN SOUTHEAST ASIAN COUNTRIES

The member states of ASEAN have very different types of governments. There are monarchies, military dictatorships, Communist systems, and multiparty democracies. The region's four monarchies are the Sultanate of Brunei, the Kingdom of Cambodia, the Federation of Malaysia, and the Kingdom of Thailand. These monarchies, except for Brunei, are constitutional monarchies in which a ruling king, queen, or sultan is a figurehead that coexists with a more democratic government that actually makes most decisions.

Myanmar, on the other hand, since 1962 has served as a clear example of a military dictatorship. Military rule is a type of nondemocratic regime where army officers seize power, either refusing to accept the rule of civilians or creating a civilian regime that they strongly influence. Often they say they are doing it for the good of the country or that they will return the country to civilian democratic rule when the time is right. The military in Thailand has also been active politically and carried out a coup against an elected government in September 2006. Thailand returned to democracy with a major national election on December 23, 2007.

Six countries in Southeast Asia—the Kingdom of Cambodia, Indonesia, the Federation of Malaysia, the Philippines, Singapore, and the Kingdom of Thailand—are multiparty, election-based democracies. In these political systems, many parties can try to win office through elections. Yet, many of these Southeast Asian democracies are not particularly strong ones. Some of the governments are plagued by corruption. There may be election irregularities. There may not be a good balance among the representative legislature, the executive branch, and an independent court system. For example, the April 2006 snap election (an election called earlier than scheduled) in Thailand was annulled because of irregularities and legal violations.

Two of the remaining five Communist countries in the world are in Southeast Asia. These Communist countries are not the sort of Communist systems associated with Soviet Communism—strict one-party rule at every level of state and society and an economy completely owned and controlled by the state. Instead, the Lao People's Democratic Republic and Vietnam have functioning parliaments where different policies are debated. However, almost all members of parliament are members of the Communist Party. Freedom of expression is limited, and the one-party system cannot be questioned. There are, however, extensive private ownership and private markets. For some in these countries, because jobs and education are open to people of all classes, a form of equality-oriented democracy exists, one with a greater priority on parity than on holding elections with many competing parties.

THE ECONOMIES OF SOUTHEAST ASIAN COUNTRIES

While Southeast Asia has some of the wealthiest economies (such as Singapore and Brunei), some of the world's poorest countries (such as Cambodia, Laos, and Myanmar) are also in this region. The region contains newly industrializing countries (NICs), developing countries where economies are growing primarily because of exports, or sales to other countries of industrial goods made in the country's factories. Thailand, Malaysia, Indonesia, the Philippines, and Vietnam have rapidly growing manufacturing sectors in which products such as hard disks for computers, basketballs, ski jackets, Nike shoes, or pickup trucks are made. Although Laos, Cambodia, and Myanmar have limited industry, are mainly agricultural, and are among the world's poorest countries, together with Vietnam they increasingly attract tourists.

Some countries in the region have more government planning and ownership, while others allow private enterprise and the market to dominate to a larger degree. Some of the Communist countries in the region tried to imitate the sort of economic planning found in the Soviet Union from the 1930s until the 1980s. But Soviet Communist Party leader Mikhail Gorbachev in the 1980s introduced changes in the Soviet economy. He called this *perestroika*, or restructuring. In 1986, Communist Vietnam and the Lao People's Democratic Republic also began to allow more private ownership and management independent of the government. In Vietnam this was called *đôi mói*.

Some of the countries that think of themselves as capitalist allow a relatively strong economic role to the state; the state may give large subsidies to private businesses, they may own some businesses or services, and they may regulate trade strictly. Thailand, for example, has a large number of strong state enterprises. Attempts to privatize these enterprises have often failed because of the resistance of the workers, who prefer the security of the existing arrangements. In December 2007, however, Thailand's Supreme Administrative Court upheld a decision to privatize PTT, Thailand's largest company and a huge energy conglomerate. Both capitalism and Communism come in different forms in Southeast Asia and around the world.

THE COUNTRIES AND PEOPLES OF ASEAN
Brunei Darussalam
Located on the northeast corner of the island of Borneo, Brunei had a special relationship with the United Kingdom until 1984. It was a protectorate, retaining its own system of government, but provided protection by the United Kingdom. After gaining full independence in 1984, Brunei became the sixth member of ASEAN.

One of the richest countries in the world, Brunei is a tax-free Muslim state. The wealth and high standard of living seen in Brunei are directly attributed to the vast amounts of oil and natural gas in the country. The Shell Oil Company, the second-largest employer in Brunei, contributes greatly to the country's economy.

Becoming a member of ASEAN was extremely important for Brunei because it is a small, resource-rich country surrounded by much larger and more powerful neighbors. ASEAN provides a security umbrella for Brunei, ensuring that it will not be invaded or taken over.

The current sultan (similar to a king) and his ancestors have ruled Brunei for six centuries. It is neither a constitutional monarchy nor a democracy, though its economic system is a free capitalist one. Most Brunei people of Malay race (the majority 67 percent of the population) work for Shell Oil or for the government. Brunei possesses abundant supplies of oil and natural gas, making it one of the richest countries in Southeast Asia and the world.

Brunei's large Chinese minority is approximately 15 percent of the population. Many temporary or "guest" workers, often from poorer Islamic countries such as Bangladesh, take lower-level jobs like driving trucks and buses.

The Kingdom of Cambodia

In various parts of the United States, such as Long Beach, San Diego, and Des Moines, there are large Cambodian communities. The presence of Cambodian-Americans results from the tragic episode of Cambodian history (1975–1978), referred to as the time of "the Killing Fields." This period produced a huge flow of refugees escaping starvation, torture, and execution. While there are approximately 172,000 Cambodian-Americans in the United States, some former refugees now have returned to Cambodia to play important roles in Cambodia's politics and economy.

This former French colony won its independence in 1953. Cambodia's Prince Sihanouk was determined to keep Cambodia neutral and out of the Vietnam War. A military coup in March 1970, allegedly supported by the United States, removed Sihanouk from power. It led to a civil war from 1970 to 1975. Extensive secret U.S. bombings of Cambodia during the earlier civil war contributed to massive suffering, death, and violence in the Cambodian countryside. This devastation and anger led to the Pol Pot regime and its killing fields. From 1975 to 1978 the extremist Communist regime of Pol Pot known as the Khmer Rouge (Red Khmer) controlled the country.

Vietnamese forces on Christmas Day in 1978, removed the Khmer Rouge from power and began a 10-year occupation. ASEAN strongly opposed the Vietnamese-supported Cambodian government as a violation of the sovereignty and self-determination of Cambodia. ASEAN convinced the United Nations not to recognize this government. Eventually, after the withdrawal of Vietnamese forces, the UN stepped in to administer a peace process (1991–1993). The peace process resulted in the return of a constitutional monarchy and democracy to Cambodia. In 2007, Cambodia had nationwide local elections that were generally considered free and fair. The free-market economy is now growing rapidly. In 1999, Cambodia became the tenth member of ASEAN.

The Republic of Indonesia

During the colonial period, Indonesia was under Dutch rule and was known as the East Indies. The Dutch East India Company established a trade economy that led to poverty and hunger among ordinary Indonesians. Improved education in response to criticisms of Dutch colonial exploitation planted the seeds for an independence movement. Sukarno (Bung Karno), one of Indonesia's revolutionary heroes who led the fight to gain independence from the Netherlands in 1949, became Indonesia's first leader. Like Prince Sihanouk of Cambodia, he wanted to be the leader of a neutral nation, siding neither with the Soviet Union nor with the United States. During the Cold War, a number of leaders of less powerful, still-developing countries wanted to remain independent of the big power blocs. Leaders and countries that preferred to avoid taking sides this way were referred to as neutralist, or nonaligned.

On September 30, 1965, in a failed attempt to seize power by the Communist Party of Indonesia (KPI), Sukarno lost power. In the middle of the night, the KPI murdered a number of key Muslim generals, creating a huge backlash in the predominantly Muslim country. General Suharto, who survived, led a successful counterattack and gradually gained control of Indonesia. A huge bloodbath, which wiped out the KPI, ensued. Suharto led Indonesia to a moderate free-market economic path. Without the political movement away from neutrality and against a strong Communist Party, Indonesia would not have become a key founding member of ASEAN two years later, in 1967. Jakarta, Indonesia, became the permanent home of the ASEAN secretariat.

Indonesia has a rich abundance of natural resources and is one of the world's leading producers of oil. It is the only Asian member of OPEC. Recent oil price increases have helped the Indonesian economy. Indonesia hosts many transnational corporations, exporting natural resources such as minerals, oil, gas, and timber, as well as sports products such as Nike shoes. The country has 10 percent of the world's tropical rain forests. Indonesia suffers from serious regional inequalities, with many in the outer remote islands complaining that their rich natural resources are exploited by the central government. Indonesia has a relatively high level of unemployment (12.5 percent) and 18 percent of its people live below the poverty line.

Indonesia's major security challenge as a country has been to maintain political stability in the face of diverse ethnic groups in the outer islands, such as the Achenese of Sumatra or the indigenous people of Irian Jaya, both pushing to become separate countries. Being part of ASEAN helps Indonesia preserve its unity.

Lao People's Democratic Republic (Lao PDR)

Many Hmong lost their lives fighting with U.S. forces against Communism in Laos during the Vietnam War. When the United States withdrew from Southeast Asia and Laos became a Communist nation, the Hmong who had supported the United States were left in a desperate situation. Many fled to refugee camps in Thailand and then migrated to the United States. Today, the upper midwestern United States, particularly Minnesota and Wisconsin, has a large population of Hmong-Americans—approximately 200,000—many of whom were born in Laos.

Laos once had a vibrant Buddhist kingdom known as Lan Xang, which means "the land of a million elephants." It was said that the Mongols with their great cavalry and horses could not defeat Lan Xang because their horses were so scared of the elephants. Lan Xang was subdivided into three smaller kingdoms and fell under Siamese control in the eighteenth century. In 1893, the French seized Laos from the Siamese, and Laos suffered serious neglect.

Laos became independent from France in 1953. Subsequently, Laos was pulled into the vortex of the Cold War and suffered from a violent civil war, which lasted until 1975 when the nation became unified and peaceful as the Lao People's Democratic

A HMONG FAMILY ODYSSEY

Yang Dao, the first Hmong person to obtain a PhD, worked as a high-ranking official in the Royal Lao Government. When Communist forces came to power in 1975, he fled to Bangkok, fearing for his future prospects and physical safety. Yang Dao explained to various embassies that the Hmong should be granted political refugee status, a designation that allows immigrants to settle legally in many countries. Although various leaders were sympathetic, many Hmong remained confined in Thai refugee camps for years.

Yang Dao and his family immigrated to France and stayed there for about seven years. While in France, he worked as a writer and journalist and wrote several books about Hmong cultural traditions. In the 1980s, Yang Dao was invited to teach Hmong language and culture at the University of Minnesota. Many Hmong now live in Minnesota, California, Wisconsin, Colorado, and North Carolina. While in Minnesota, Dr. Yang Dao also worked in the multicultural office of the St. Paul Public School District to help the public schools respond to the special needs of new immigrant groups from Southeast Asia. During this period he wrote *Hmong at the Turning Point* (1993).

Dr. Yang Dao has a large extended family in the United States. His sister Blia Yang also lives in Minnesota and raised nine successful

Republic, a Communist nation. During the chaotic period prior to 1975, Laos became the most heavily bombed country in the history of the world. Many unexploded weapons remain in some remote parts of Laos; many innocent rural dwellers have died when the weapons were accidentally triggered.

In 1986, Laos followed Vietnam's lead and introduced new free economic market mechanisms to improve its economy.

children as a single mother. One of her daughters, May yer Theresa Ly-Thao, became the first Hmong woman president of the Hmong Minnesota Student Association at the University of Minnesota. She also joined the Peace Corps and served in Thailand. While she was in Thailand, the United States decided that the Hmong refugees at refugee camp Wat Tham Krabok could resettle in the United States. May yer was hired to work as a cultural orientation trainer at the refugee camp to help the Hmong refugees prepare for resettlement in the United States. One of May yer's sisters, Maychy Vu, is director of HOPE Community Academy in St. Paul, Minnesota, the first Hmong charter school in the United States.

Hmong-Americans are the fastest-growing group of Southeast Asian immigrants in the United States. The Hmong community in Minnesota has become so large that they need to rent the Metrodome, home of the NFL Minnesota Vikings, for their annual New Year's celebration. An annual Hmong Sports Festival in early July in St. Paul, Minnesota, attracts Hmong from around the world. Approximately 12,000 Hmong veterans are honored on Veteran's Day. The late Minnesota senator Paul Wellstone worked tirelessly on behalf of his Hmong constituents, particularly working for the rights of Hmong veterans of the war in Southeast Asia.

Beginning in the 1990s, Laos became actively involved with the world economy. It became a member of ASEAN in 1997 and now has good global relations and receives extensive development assistance from the World Bank, Asian Development Bank, Japan, the EU, Switzerland, the Scandinavian countries, and the Arab world. Despite considerable economic growth in recent years, Laos remains one of the world's poorest economies.

Federation of Malaysia

When John F. Kennedy became president in 1960, one of his major policies was to improve opportunities for disadvantaged groups. Some of these policies later became what is now called affirmative action, designed to assist many disadvantaged ethnic groups, including African Americans, Native Americans, and Latinos. A few years later, soon after the formation of ASEAN, Malaysia initiated a bold program to help its disadvantaged *bumiputra*, or "children of the soil"—local, largely rural Malay people who lagged economically and educationally far behind their urban Chinese and Indian neighbors. The initiative was called the New Economic Policy. It is probably the world's most dramatic example of a broad-based, successful affirmative-action program. The initiative significantly helped the disadvantaged local Malay population to improve their educational and occupational opportunities.

The roots of Malaysia's current ethnic diversity and related issues can be found in the country's colonial history. Since most of the Malays were traditional farmers, the British found it necessary to import Chinese and Indian laborers to work in the tin mines and on the rubber plantations. Thus, Malaysia now has a large Chinese population and also a sizeable Indian population, making it a culturally diverse nation.

Malaysia was a founding member of ASEAN and one of the three original members of the Association of Southeast Asia (ASA), which was the precursor to ASEAN. Malaysia is comprised of two parts, western peninsular Malaysia and eastern island Malaysia, which includes two states, Sabah and Sarawak, on the northern part of the large island of Borneo. Western peninsular Malaysia has a northern border with Thailand, and the small island nation of Singapore is to the immediate south. Peninsular Malaysia is a "landbridge" between mainland and island Southeast Asia.

Malaysia is a constitutional monarchy, and each of its 13 states has a sultan. The monarch's role is mainly symbolic and ceremonial, and Malaysia operates as a parliamentary democracy. Its parliament has two chambers. The main political party has held power with smaller allies since 1957, and ethnic Malays dominate politics. Malaysia operates as a federal system, with each state having considerable authority of its own.

Among Southeast Asian economies, Malaysia's success has been second only to Singapore. It has a highly diversified economy with an abundance of natural resources such as palm oil, rubber, and tin, along with a strong manufacturing and emerging high technology sector (the Multimedia Super Corridor). It is one of the new Asian Tigers. This term originally referred to Hong Kong, Singapore, South Korea, and Taiwan—all of which grew rapidly between the 1960s and 1990s. Now, with growth rates high in Indonesia, the Philippines, Thailand, and Malaysia, they too could be considered Asian Tigers. These eight countries are geographically close to the economic giants Japan, China, and India.

The state has played an important role in Malaysia's capitalist economy. Its affirmative-action program has served to reduce inequality. During the 1997 Asian economic crisis, Malaysia was the only Asian economy that did not seek financial assistance from the International Monetary Fund. It aims to become a fully developed nation by the year 2020.

The country has a diverse population comprised primarily of Malays (50.4 percent), Chinese (23.7 percent), indigenous peoples (11.1 percent), and Indians (7.1 percent). Its Malay population is primarily Muslim. Ethnic relations have been relatively good, but recently there has been concern over ethnic segregation and other related tensions.

The Union of Myanmar (formerly Burma)

In September 2007, thousands of people took to the streets to peacefully protest the Myanmar military government's increases in the price of oil and gas and its undemocratic nature. Leading the demonstrations were Buddhist monks, who enjoy great honor in the society. Demonstrators, including monks, were killed, injured, and arrested. Many tried to flee the country. Both the international community and ASEAN condemned the repression.

Formerly a British colony and part of "Greater India," Burma gained independence in 1947. It seemed to be creating a workable form of democratic federalism that would give significant local power to various ethnic communities. However, Burma's leader at the time, the charismatic and dynamic Aung San, was assassinated in 1947. Since 1962, Myanmar has had a military dictatorship that has isolated the country from the rest of the world. Aung San Suu Kyi, the daughter of Aung San, put Myanmar back on the world map with her struggle to bring democracy to the country. She won the Nobel Peace Prize in 1991, but she has often been under house arrest by the Burmese military regime.

Like Indonesia and Laos, Myanmar has tremendous ethnic diversity. Only about 68 percent of the country's population is ethnically Burman. The Union of Myanmar remains one of the poorest countries in the world. Though it is not a Communist country, the state, dominated by the military, plays an important role in the economy. Historically, prior to military rule, Myanmar was one of the world's leading exporters of rice. Its current poverty is explained by years of isolation and the inefficiency of the military-dominated state-run economy.

ASEAN admitted Myanmar in 1997 as a way of trying to engage its military rulers, move the country toward greater

In September 2007, despite participating in nonviolent protests against difficult economic conditions and military rule, Buddhist monks and other demonstrators were killed, injured, or arrested by the police. Harsh tactics are commonly used by the military-run government.

respect for human rights, and to provide a better voice for its population. Especially after the events of fall 2007, Myanmar's membership remains controversial.

The Republic of the Philippines

Roughly one percent of the U.S. population, or nearly 3 million people, are Filipino-Americans. They make up the largest group of Americans with Southeast Asian heritage and are concentrated in California and Hawaii. Since the Philippines were once a U.S. colony, many Filipinos are fluent in English. Many of the more educated have moved overseas to work as doctors, nurses, teachers, and in other professions, contributing to a serious "brain drain," or emigration of the trained and talented to other places. In addition, many Filipinos have emigrated to work as maids in Hong Kong and Saudi Arabia, to work in the entertainment industry in Japan, or to work on cruise ships. Such workers often send money back to their families, a valuable and growing source of hard currency for the country.

At the end of World War II, in 1946, the Philippines obtained its independence from the United States. The Philippines established a system of political democracy modeled after the U.S. presidential system. This democratic period ended with the notorious dictatorship of Ferdinand Marcos, who subsequently was thrown out of office by "people power" in February 1986. There was a huge popular uprising (with the Catholic Church playing a major role) against Marcos's government, triggered by the assassination of opposition leader Benigno "Ninoy" Aquino in 1983. Supporters of Ninoy convinced his wife, Corazon, to enter into politics as head of the Laban Party, which was set up to back Corazon Aquino in the presidential election. Initially, Aquino was to run for vice president, but one million signatures were gathered in one week for her to run for president. After the elections, Marcos claimed victory, but the elections were believed to be rigged, and Marcos fled the country in the face of huge nonviolent demonstrations, military opposition, and U.S. pressure. Corazon Aquino served as president from 1986 to 1992 and Fidel Ramos, one of Marcos's former generals who had joined the opposition against Marcos and was a key figure in the demonstrations that led to Marcos's exile, later followed Aquino as president of the Philippines. Following the overthrow of Marcos, and on the request of the Philippine government, the United States withdrew its military forces from the Philippines' Clark and Subic Bay bases. With its bases removed, the United States now has much less influence in the Philippines.

Massive national debt, government corruption, coup attempts, a Communist insurgency, and a Muslim separatist movement have tempered the positive developments of 1986. Although the economy improved under President Fidel Ramos (1992–1998), the East Asian financial crisis in 1997 and allegations of corruption and election rigging have hounded the Philippine government. From 2002 to 2006 the Philippines experienced robust economic growth on an average of 5 percent a year, but control of the economy by the wealthy and landowning class continues to be a serious issue. High levels of inequality persist, with 40 percent of Filipinos living below the poverty line.

The Republic of Singapore

One of the founding members of ASEAN, Singapore is a former British colony and was briefly part of Malaysia (1963–1965). A small island located off the southern coast of Malaysia near Indonesia's northwestern islands, it is one of the few remaining city-states and the smallest country in Southeast Asia.

While trying to be self-sufficient after becoming independent in 1965, the fledgling nation experienced mass unemployment, housing shortages, and a dearth of land and natural resources. During the administration of Lew Kuan Yew, who served as prime minister from 1959 to 1990, the foundation of the country's economic infrastructure was developed. Today, with an estimated GDP per capita of $48,900 in 2007, Singapore is the richest country in Southeast Asia and the most technologically advanced.[4]

Singapore is a major world and Pacific port located in the geographic center of Southeast Asia. It is also close to the major and vital shipping routes connecting Asia, Europe, and the Middle East. Singapore competes with Hong Kong and Shanghai to be the most important Asia-Pacific port. It is a major center of international trade, investments, and communications. Singapore may have benefited the most of any country from its ASEAN membership because it was best positioned to take advantage of ASEAN's increasingly free trade.

On the surface, Singapore has a parliamentary democracy with many political parties. In actuality, politics in Singapore has been dominated by the People's Action Party (PAP), so much so that many observers regard Singapore as more authoritarian than democratic. Laws that restrict freedom of speech are justified by saying that free speech will lead to ill will or disharmony in Singapore's multiethnic society. The courts are not strongly independent of the party and other parts of the government. Nevertheless, former prime minister Lee Kuan Yew and PAP created an extremely stable political system with a well-trained professional civil service.

In 1993, the island nation of Singapore became a focus in U.S. newspapers when Michael Fay, an American teenager living there, pled guilty to vandalizing cars and stealing road signs. Under the 1966 Singapore Vandalism Act he was sentenced to four months in jail, a fine of about $2,000, and six strokes of a cane. Many Americans condemned the punishment, especially the caning, as too severe, and President Bill Clinton pressured the government to withdraw the caning. Michael Fay's punishment was decreased from six to four lashes, but the Singapore government and much of Southeast Asia were shocked by U.S. interference with their process of law.

The Kingdom of Thailand (formerly Siam)

Like the United States, Thailand, formerly known as Siam, opened its doors to migrants primarily in the nineteenth century. In fact, *Thailand* means "land of the free." Thailand, one of the founding members of ASEAN, is the only Southeast Asian nation never to have been a colony, as it was able to maneuver skillfully between the British and French, both of which had designs on its territory.

In 1939, the country changed its name from Siam to Thailand. During World War II, Thailand became an ally of Japan. Joining with Japan, while a Free Thai movement simultaneously supported the Allies, protected Thailand, which suffered the fewest lost lives and the least damage of any country in Southeast Asia. Their clever use of diplomacy also helped save Thailand from being punished after the war for having been an ally of Japan.

In the postwar period, Thailand became a strong ally of the United States. It allowed the United States use of its military bases to wage war against Communist forces in Vietnam, Laos, and Cambodia. Thailand became a huge "land aircraft carrier."

Thailand had one of the hottest economies in the world in the 1980s and 1990s. Due to outside pressures, Thailand allowed funds to flow freely into and out of the country. As a result the Thai private sector acquired a burden of international debt. In addition, on July 2, 1997, Thailand allowed its currency, the baht, to float (the exchange rate or values against other currencies fluctuate in line with supply and demand in the free market) instead of remaining fixed. The value of the baht was quickly cut in half, creating a huge burden for investors. This led to the Asian financial crisis, which rapidly spread to other Asian countries and raised fears of a worldwide economic meltdown. Like other Asia-Pacific and Southeast Asian economies, Thailand has experienced an impressive economic recovery from the crisis.

During his time as prime minister (2001–2006), Dr. Thaksin Shinawatra's policies improved conditions in disadvantaged rural areas of the north and northeast, where he retains significant political popularity. The northeast remains, however, the country's most disadvantaged area and major regional disparities persist.

There are 143,169 Thai-Americans. One of the most famous is professional golfer Tiger Woods, whose mother is from Thailand. New York Yankees baseball star Johnny Damon also has a mother from Thailand. Sixty-six percent of Thai-Americans live in Los Angeles, which has the world's only Thai Town. Los Angeles, like Bangkok (the capital of Thailand), literally means "City of Angels."

Socialist Republic of Vietnam

One of the most famous images of the Vietnam War is of a naked young Vietnamese girl running from a village, her body inflamed with napalm (a flammable liquid used in warfare) and her face contorted with pain. That photograph, taken by Nick Ut, displayed to the whole world the horrors of the Vietnam War. Kim Phúc, the girl from the photo, now is a Canadian citizen living in Ottawa with her husband and two children,[5] and runs a foundation to help child victims of war. Kim's success and inspiring story reflects the resilience of the Vietnamese both at home and abroad in the face of the tragedy of war, death, and violence.

From 1975 to 1985, a vast number of Vietnamese refugees (often called boat people) left Vietnam for the United States. Currently there are more than 1.4 million Vietnamese-Americans living in the United States. Representing 0.5 percent of the U.S. population, they are the second-largest Southeast Asian–American group in the United States.

Much attention has focused on the military conflict in Vietnam and the war there. However, Vietnam is more than just a war. For example, Vietnamese art has a long, rich history, dating back to the creation of pottery at about the time of the Stone Age. Silk painting once was one of the most popular art forms in Vietnam. Artists used liberal amounts of color, which differentiated their works from those of the Chinese and Japanese, and they typically painted the countryside, historical events, or scenes of daily life. Vietnamese architecture is noted for its Chinese, and later French, influence. Vietnamese films date back to the 1920s and have been shaped largely by wars fought there from the 1940s to the 1970s. Recent years have seen films depicting the nightlife of the capital, Ho Chi Minh City, while also warning of the dangers of HIV/AIDS.

Vietnam is one of the five remaining Communist countries in the world. It is a one-party state with the Communist Party dominating politics and policies. Opposition to the one-party state is

During the Vietnam War, Kim Phúc *(above)* became famous when a military photographer snapped a picture of her running down a road, covered in burning chemicals. Despite its rich culture and history, Vietnam, like several other Southeast Asian countries, is known more for violent conflicts than for its contributions to the international arena.

not tolerated, though within the country's National Assembly there are often policy debates and differences.

With the unification of Vietnam in 1975 and the introduction of "*đổi mới*" (private free market economic mechanisms) in 1986, Vietnam has made impressive economic gains and is a rising phoenix on the world economic scene. Vietnam has greatly reduced the number of state-owned businesses and has opened its economy to trade with much of the world. Vietnam normalized relations with the United States in 1995, became a member of ASEAN in 1997, a member of the Asia-Pacific Economic Cooperation forum (APEC) in 1998, and a member of the World Trade Organization (WTO) in 2007. Since 1996, trade between the United States and Vietnam has expanded by roughly 900 percent. Between 2005 and 2007, Vietnam was the fastest growing economy in the ASEAN region and one of the hottest economies in the Asia-Pacific region.

The History
and Evolution
of ASEAN

THE DEVELOPMENT OF ASEAN WAS BUILT ON OTHER ATTEMPTS in the region to bring countries together for cooperation. The Southeast Asia Treaty Organization (SEATO), established in 1954 by the Southeast Asia Collective Defense Treaty or the Manila Pact, was one of the first examples of regional cooperation in Southeast Asia. It was established under Western auspices with the United States playing the leading role. Its members included Australia, France, New Zealand, Pakistan, the Philippines, Thailand, the United Kingdom, and the United States. It was mainly a collective defense system, created to block further Communist gains in Southeast Asia. This was similar to the idea behind the North Atlantic Treaty Organization (NATO), in which the military forces of each member would provide a collective defense against outside forces.

SEATO was unable to reach unanimous decisions on whether to intervene in the conflicts in Cambodia, Laos, and Vietnam. The organization later disbanded in 1977.

Another attempt at regional cooperation to achieve security was the Association of Southeast Asia (ASA), which operated from 1961 to 1967. Europe's response to the tragedy and disaster of two horrific world wars was the inspiration for the development of this regional organization. In March 1957, through the Treaty of Rome, the European Economic Community (EEC) was established, inspired by the vision of the French leader and thinker Jean Monnet.[6] Four years later ASA was born.

The major rationale for regional cooperation in Southeast Asia continued to be security and defense against Communist invasion and revolution. By 1961, not only had China and the North Koreans invaded South Korea, but Communist forces in North Vietnam had decisively defeated the French in 1954 with the clear goal of reunifying the country under their rule. The world Communist movement was supporting local Communist groups in the Philippines, Malaysia, Thailand, Singapore, Burma, and Indonesia. In fact, the Communist Party of Indonesia (PKI) was to become the world's second-largest Communist party after the Chinese one.

Except for Indonesia, all of the Southeast Asian countries are relatively small. Working together they could become stronger economically. To lessen the appeal of Communism they needed to strengthen social and economic development and not squander resources fighting among themselves. Leaders also wanted to contain Indonesia, by far Southeast Asia's largest power, which had designs on the resource-rich western part of the island of New Guinea, the island of East Timor, and parts of Borneo controlled by Malaysia and Brunei.

ASA had only three members: Malaysia, the Philippines, and Thailand. Tunku Abdul Rahman Putra Al-Haj, prime minister of Malaysia, is generally credited with initiating the idea of

ASA.[7] A declaration creating the organization was announced in Bangkok, Thailand, on July 31, 1961, at a meeting of the foreign ministers of the three countries. Though the key reason for the creation of ASA was security, the formal official declaration placed greater emphasis on economic and social cooperation.

ASA had a rough start. Soon after its formation, the Philippines made claims to Sabah, an area off the island of Borneo that was to become part of the new Federation of Malaysia, creating tension between the Philippines and Malaysia. The Thais, drawing on the diplomatic skills of their foreign minister, Dr. Thanat Khoman, worked hard to restore harmony to ASA, and by March 1966, ASA was functioning well despite what had been a temporary interruption in good relations.

Though in concrete terms ASA accomplished little, it was important for two reasons. First, it led to extensive communication among the three participating nations, providing Thailand the opportunity to employ its diplomacy to help resolve the Philippine-Malaysian dispute over Sabah. Second, ASA kept alive the idea of a Southeast Asian regional cooperative organization originating in the region itself and not sponsored by outsiders.[8]

MAPHILINDO

MAPHILINDO (MAlaya, PHILippines, INDOnesia), another regional organization, was established in July 1963. Filipino nationalist hero and intellectual José Rizal dreamed of uniting the Malay peoples, who were divided by the colonial powers. MAPHILINDO brought together the Malay peoples of Malaya, the Philippines, and Indonesia. The predominant populations of these nations share a common racial/ethnic Malay identity, and their languages are related. Indonesia, the largest country in the region, participated for the first time in a regional cooperative body. Later, Indonesia was a key player in the formation and management of ASEAN. Actually, MAPHILINDO's significance lies not in its accomplishments, per se, but in its ability to involve Indonesia in regional activities and to bring together nations that had serious conflicts over territorial claims.

THE BEGINNINGS OF ASEAN

ASEAN grew out of ASA. Thailand's role in eliminating the conflict and disputes among Indonesia, Malaysia, and the Philippines during the days of ASA and MAPHILINDO led to the realization that regional cooperation could become a reality and could contribute to peace and harmony in the region. Dr. Thanat Khoman, the only surviving statesman from those days, provides insight into the beginnings of ASEAN:

> At the banquet marking the reconciliation between the three disputants, I broached the idea of forming another organization for regional cooperation with Adam Malik [the Indonesia foreign minister after the Sukarno era]. Malik agreed without hesitation but asked for time to talk with his government and also to normalize relations with Malaysia now that the confrontation was over. Meanwhile, the Thai Foreign Office prepared a draft charter of the new institution. Within a few months everything was ready. I therefore invited the two former members of the Association for Southeast Asia (ASA), Malaysia, and the Philippines, and Indonesia, a key member, to a meeting in Bangkok.[9]

In an April 2007 interview at the age of 93, Dr. Thanat emphasized that a major rationale for the formation of ASEAN was to achieve greater strength through unity in relation to the large external powers and to achieve harmony among the countries of the region.[10]

In early August 1967, the foreign ministers of Indonesia, Malaysia, the Philippines, Thailand, and Singapore met for

In 1967, five key Southeast Asian leaders met in Bangkok to sign the ASEAN Declaration. From left to right: Narciso Ramos, Philippine foreign secretary; Adam Malik, Indonesian foreign minister; Thanat Khoman, Thai foreign minister; Abdul Razak, Malaysian deputy premier; and Sinnathamby Rajaratnam, Singapore foreign minister. The leaders hoped the formation of another regional organization would maintain friendly relations among member countries.

four days at the quiet beach resort of Bang Saen, southeast of Bangkok, to work out details of the declaration to create ASEAN. Negotiations took place in a highly informal and cordial manner, described as "sports-shirt diplomacy." While the ministers met to conduct business, they also took time to play golf and eat Thai food, and much goodwill and good humor were in evidence. This informal and friendly way of negotiating became part of the ASEAN tradition.[11]

After the informal meetings at Bang Saen, the five leaders met officially in Bangkok on August 8, 1967, to sign what has become known as the ASEAN Declaration, sometimes referred to as the Bangkok Declaration. The five foreign ministers, considered ASEAN's founding fathers, who signed the document were: Adam Malik of Indonesia, Narciso R. Ramos of the Philippines, Tun Abdul Razak of Malaysia, S. Rajaratnam of Singapore, and Dr. Thanat Khoman of Thailand. The declaration is a simple, two-page document

THE ASEAN SYMBOL

The ASEAN symbol is a blue background with a red and white circle surrounding ten stalks of yellow rice plants. The circle represents the unity of the ASEAN countries. The ten stalks of rice represent the original dream of ASEAN's founding fathers of an organization made up of all ten nations of the region living in friendship, solidarity, and harmony. These four colors—blue, red, white, and yellow—represent the main colors of the crests of all the ASEAN countries. Each color also has a more general significance: blue represents peace and stability, red stands for courage and dynamism, yellow represents prosperity, and white represents purity. Thus, the symbol refers to ASEAN's objectives of unity, peace, stability, courage, dynamism, purity, and prosperity. The ASEAN flag is the symbol on a solid blue background.

The prominent place of rice on ASEAN's symbol reflects the importance of agriculture in the region and the tradition of cooperative wet rice culture. Cooperative wet rice culture, which dates back centuries, is a practice of farmers joining together to produce and harvest rice planted in shallows pools of water.

with only five parts or articles. It proclaimed that ASEAN represented "the collective will of the nations of Southeast Asia to bind themselves together in friendship and cooperation and, through joint efforts and sacrifices, secure for their peoples and for posterity the blessings of peace, freedom and prosperity."[12]

The initial ASEAN Declaration signed in 1967 indicated that the organization was open to all Southeast Asian nations. Because leaders have valued regional unity over specific ways

Malaysian Foreign Minister Abdullah Ahmad Badawi answers questions in front of the ASEAN flag on May 31, 1997. That day ASEAN agreed to admit Myanmar, Laos, and Cambodia into the organization.

of doing politics or structuring economies, ASEAN has no specific requirements for membership. It has focused more on nonintervention than requiring democracy or respect for human rights among new and continuing members.

ASEAN, 1960s to 2004

ASEAN was created primarily from fear of the spread of Communism. From the 1960s to the early 1980s, the external threat of Communism loomed, and the need for unity and solidarity among the non-Communist Southeast Asian nations was of major importance. On November 27, 1971, in Kuala Lumpur, Malaysia, ASEAN approved the Zone of Peace, Freedom, and Neutrality Declaration (ZOPFA), which stressed that countries should be free of outside interference and that the region should be an area free of conflict. With the military withdrawal of both the United Kingdom and the United States from the region in the late 1960s; the eventual victory of Communism in Vietnam, Laos, and Cambodia in 1975; and the intervention of the Vietnamese military in Cambodia in 1978, ASEAN provided security for the non-Communist countries of Southeast Asia. Peace, harmony, and the end of conflicts among the Southeast Asian nations were major themes of this period.

Economic development and economic conflicts characterized ASEAN's next stage of evolution, from the 1980s to 1997. The rise in power of Japan and the competition for its investments were defining elements of this period. It was during this phase, in 1992, that AFTA (ASEAN Free Trade Area) was approved, reflecting a serious commitment to deeper and broader economic cooperation among the countries of the region.

The third phase of ASEAN's evolution was ushered in by the Asian financial crisis in 1997, an economic shock heard around the world. It started in Thailand when the government allowed its currency to change value according to the free market. In only a few weeks, the Thai currency lost half its value.

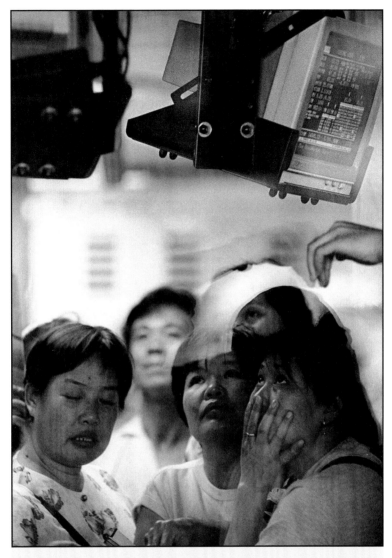

When the value of Thai currency took a tumble, it affected entire economies as well as many private investors in Asia *(above)*. ASEAN quickly responded by establishing the ASEAN Plus Three forum. With the involvement of its member countries and three of the continent's most powerful nations—China, Japan, and South Korea—ASEAN Plus Three created projects that would help stimulate the economies of all its participants.

Soon the crisis spread to other Asian countries including Korea, Indonesia, the Philippines, Malaysia, and eventually Laos.

This crisis created the need for ASEAN to think seriously about financial cooperation. After the crisis, a forum called ASEAN Plus Three (members of ASEAN and the three East Asian nations of China, South Korea, and Japan) initiated several projects to enhance financial cooperation. Among these were bilateral swaps—arrangements between two countries to lend to each other on different terms, such as exchanging one country's lower fixed interest rate for another's lower floating interest rate. Each of these countries then is able to take advantage of the other's lower rates or assets. For example, soon after the financial crisis, Indonesia helped Thailand to meet its international debt obligations. It was able to do so primarily because it was a major oil producer. ASEAN also began to respond to the external economic challenges posed by the rise in stature of China and India, each with over a billion people. ASEAN's geographic location, exactly between these two economic powers, made economic competitiveness extremely important. Although some believe that ASEAN Plus Three's significance has been eclipsed by the East Asia Summit (a pan-Asia forum established in 2005 and held annually by the leaders of 16 Asian countries and the region, with ASEAN in the leadership position), the East Asia Summit is the group that has been credited with creating the basis for financial stability in Asia; the lack of such stability contributed to the Asian financial crisis.

The fourth phase of ASEAN's evolution dates from the tragic events of September 11, 2001, when extremist Muslims flew airplanes into the Twin Towers in New York City, igniting global concern over international terrorism. The members of ASEAN at the Eighth ASEAN Summit in Phnom Penh, Cambodia, on November 3, 2002, drafted and approved the Declaration on Terrorism. The ASEAN countries agreed to intensify their cooperative efforts to combat terrorism, a new kind of security concern.

At the Twelfth ASEAN Summit in Cebu, Philippines, in January 2007, ASEAN members agreed on an accelerated schedule for achieving an ASEAN Economic Community. They hope to do this by 2015. In November 2007, ASEAN members signed a new charter pointing in this direction. Members also signed ASEAN free trade agreements with other Asian economic powers such as Japan, China, and India—agreements that would result in the dismantling of tariffs between all ASEAN countries and these large trading partners. The signing of an agreement between ASEAN and China in 2002 to work toward a free trade area is particularly noteworthy because of the size of the Chinese market. Cooperation related to tourism, with many implications for economic, social, and cultural development, is also an important element of ASEAN in its current and final phase.

In the new charter signed in 2007, ASEAN signaled a new emphasis on a broader range of concerns. Like many other regional and global organizations, it has begun to talk about human security, as well as the security of the nation-state. Rather than focusing on whether states are able to exercise their sovereignty without interference, ASEAN is looking at a range of concerns about the well-being of people and their communities. This shift in emphasis has been possible because of the end of the Cold War. The 1997 Asian economic crisis, which caused widespread insecurity among investors, also highlighted the importance of human security, as did the Indian Ocean tsunami of 2004 and the SARS and bird flu epidemics of 2003–2004.

ASEAN has plans to set up a Human Rights Commission, though the charter does not set the scope and powers of the commission. Observers think that the provision is weak because of the opposition and human rights abuses of the military regime in Myanmar. Nevertheless, ASEAN has begun to say officially that it expects countries to meet basic human rights standards.

ASEAN AS A REGIONAL ORGANIZATION

In 1997, on the thirtieth anniversary of ASEAN, its leaders agreed on a shared vision of ASEAN as "a concert of Southeast Asian nations, outward looking, living in peace, stability and prosperity, bonded together in partnership in dynamic development and in a community of caring societies."[13] In 2003, ASEAN leaders resolved to create an ASEAN community based on three key ideas—maintaining peace and secure borders, promoting economic growth and prosperity, and fostering the cultural richness of the region. In November 2007, ASEAN celebrated its fortieth anniversary and signed a new charter, aspiring to not only closer economic cooperation but also to becoming a "community of caring societies." ASEAN has adapted to dramatic changes in global developments. It is quite a different organization now compared to four decades ago when it was founded. Once concerned mainly with issues of security, it now focuses on social and economic growth and development.

During its four decades of existence, increasing interdependence has also been a defining characteristic of ASEAN. Trade among the countries of the region has significantly increased. The Asian economic crisis quickly spread from Thailand to its ASEAN neighbors. The intense smog generated by fires on the island of Borneo (Indonesia's Kalimantan area) and Sumatra in 2003 adversely affected Singapore, Malaysia, and southern Thailand. Thailand, with its rapidly aging population and extremely low fertility rate, is increasingly in need of immigrant labor from neighboring areas such as Cambodia, Laos, and Myanmar. With an accelerated schedule to achieve an ASEAN Economic Community by the year 2015, economic interdependence will steadily intensify.

Among world and regional organizations, ASEAN has an excellent record for its consensus-style decision making and its smooth and effective operation. It has had impressive unity and solidarity in its approach to nonmembers around the region and the globe. However, it remains an

intergovernmental regional organization. An intergovernmental organization is an association of nation-states that
agree to collaborate in political, economic, and cultural areas.
However, each country in ASEAN retains control over its own
policies. Intergovernmental organizations' powers are weak in
the sense that the organization itself cannot force countries
to carry out its rules. They also do not employ many people to
develop policies in the interests of the region as a whole or
to enforce policies. Conversely, stronger regional organizations, such as the European Union, have institutions that pass
laws that are binding on member countries.

The twentieth century was dominated by wars waged
between nation-states. Between 170 million and 220 million
people were killed in wars. The regional grouping of states,
such as ASEAN and the European Union, an organization of
27 countries in Europe, appears to be an alternative to violent
conflicts. ASEAN has so far emphasized diplomacy to prevent conflict and free trade rather than economic and social
development within its member states. One of its challenges is
uniting and building cooperation in a geographical region with
great political, economic, and cultural diversity. States in these
regional groupings agree to form a special organization and
follow particular rules that will govern how they behave toward
each other and other areas in the world. These kinds of groups
encourage nation-states to connect with and rely on each other.
They develop ways of resolving their disagreements through
peaceful political debate and negotiation. This is sometimes
called cooperative interdependence.

Possible conflicts among nation-states can be resolved
peacefully within such regional frameworks. As such regional
bodies become more effective, the need for national military
spending for defense and security may diminish. For example,
within the Central American Common Market (CACM), the
nation of Costa Rica has no military forces because it belongs
to a regional organization that makes it feel secure. It trusts

its neighbors. The strengthening of international and regional groups could help turn "swords into ploughs" and improve the quality of life and happiness for all.

For example, with the collapse of the Soviet Union, the Communist Southeast Asian nations of Vietnam and Laos were forced to rethink their international policies and strategies. They could no longer count on receiving major subsidies and economic assistance from the Soviet Union and the former Eastern bloc. On February 3, 1994, President Clinton lifted the trade embargo against Vietnam, and on July 11, 1995, the United States normalized relations with Vietnam. Just 17 days later, on July 28, Vietnam became the seventh member of ASEAN.

Subsequently, in 1997, the Lao People's Democratic Republic and the Union of Myanmar became the eighth and ninth members of ASEAN. In 1999, the Kingdom of Cambodia became the tenth member of ASEAN. The next potential member of ASEAN is East Timor (Democratic Republic of Timor-Leste), which became a new sovereign nation on May 20, 2002. From 1975 to 2000, it had been a province of Indonesia. A popular uprising led to a referendum in 1999 in which the people voted for independence.

As of January 1, 2003, many tariffs had been removed to make ASEAN a free trade area. It will probably become a completely free trade area by 2010. Countries belonging to free trade areas have eliminated tariffs, or taxes on imported goods, coming from other countries within the organization. But individual countries still set tariffs on goods coming from countries outside of the organization and region.

Ranking among the world's most important free trade areas, Southeast Asia is an important part of the world economy. Compared with other major regional groupings, such as the European Union and NAFTA, ASEAN is second in terms of population, fourth in the number of member states, and fifth in total GDP. Given the economic dynamism of many of its members, ASEAN is likely to grow in importance and significance in the new century.

Because of their close proximity and ability to provide various resources, the member countries of ASEAN have been encouraged to create agreements that would address the economic and social needs of each nation. In 1997, ASEAN raised the Lao and Burmese flags *(above)* at the site of a meeting, signifying their acceptance into the organization. Their membership, as well as the upcoming acceptance of East Timor, will increase interregional trade and economic development.

ASEAN is also moving toward being an economic community, with a higher level of economic cooperation. It is going beyond just removing tariffs to developing other rules that would allow people, wealth, and goods to move freely among its members. It is also discussing the possibility of becoming a customs union; instead of each country setting a tariff for its outside trade, ASEAN would take over setting tariffs on goods coming from outside the member countries. While almost every country in ASEAN still has its own banking system and currency, Singapore and Brunei have a monetary union, sharing a central bank and currency.

How ASEAN Works

ASEAN BEGAN AS A GROUP OF FIVE DIVERSE NATIONS— Indonesia, Malaysia, the Philippines, Thailand, and Singapore—seeking to cooperate as a way to protect one another from the regional threat of Communism and to minimize conflict and division within the region. These five nations had quite different histories, and their political systems and economies varied. The countries that joined the original five—Brunei, Vietnam, Laos, Myanmar, and Cambodia—have added yet more differences.

Despite these dramatic differences among ASEAN countries, they have worked together using a consensus decision-making approach. A consensus agreement is one that is reached after people with different interests and points of view discuss a problem and find a resolution that seems the best for all. It does not mean that everyone agrees at the beginning. The resolution is one that is genuinely accepted and will stand as an agreed decision for a long period of time. Unlike a situation of majority voting, consensus decisions mean that the disagreement of just one country among many can doom a decision. In addition to ASEAN members making decisions in which all agree, they have sometimes agreed to disagree.

The flexible ASEAN consensus process is based on the Malay and Indonesian village cultural practices of *musyawarah* and *mufakat*.[14] *Musyawarah* refers to consultative leadership where the leader consults broadly before making a decision. Integral to the concept is the notion that every voice must be heard.[15] *Mufakat* means "consensus," the goal of musyawarah. This is also similar to what the Japanese call *nemawashi*. This style of decision making also reflects the ideals of wet rice cooperative culture common to many countries of Southeast Asia. There are three key principles related to ASEAN's successful style, namely, the three Rs: restraint, respect, and responsibility.[16] This represents a special Asian way of conducting international relations. Thus, the ASEAN way emphasizes harmony, solidarity, and avoiding any direct face-to-face conflict.

In addition, a guiding principle of ASEAN decision making has been to refrain from interfering in the domestic affairs of any member state and noninterference among countries. Without this principle, it is unlikely that ASEAN, comprised of countries with widely differing political and economic systems, would have survived.

More recently, however, consensus and noninterference have been called into question. In the ASEAN charter adopted in November 2007, a provision states that members can make agreements that some may decide not to sign. These sorts of agreements may be necessary on issues of crime across borders, refugees fleeing countries like Myanmar, and trade. In addition, a Human Rights Commission has been added to ASEAN's organizational structure. Rather than leaving issues of human rights to individual countries, ASEAN seems to be moving toward a principle that it has the right to demand certain human rights standards from its members.

Over the years, there have been many agreements to guide the work of ASEAN and its members. These agreements may be treaties, declarations, statements, or communiqués. Technically, in international legal terms, a treaty is a stronger agreement. However, within the ASEAN context, these are simply basic agreements to cooperate in accord with the declaration or statement. Two important examples of such agreements and declarations are the Zone of Peace, Freedom and Neutrality Declaration (Kuala Lumpur, November 27, 1971) and the ASEAN Free Trade Area (AFTA) agreement made at the 1992 ASEAN Summit in Singapore. The first declaration stated that the ASEAN region was to be a zone of neutrality free of any external interference by outside powers. The second historic agreement on AFTA was the decision to move toward a free trade area by eliminating or reducing tariffs on each other's products. However, there is no regional governing structure or court system to force countries to abide by such treaties and declarations, nor any way to punish countries for failure to comply.

ASEAN basically provides a systematic way for leaders and major officials of the Southeast Asian member countries to come together on a regular basis to discuss, face-to-face, major issues in the region. Thus, it is a "talking body," and its basic activity is hundreds of meetings each year. Critics see ASEAN as a social organization offering mostly talk, not action, with many parties, receptions, and golf for the elites of the participating nations with little benefit for the ordinary people. However, ASEAN, despite its loose organizational structure, has had a number of impressive accomplishments.

SUMMITS

The first ASEAN summit involving the heads of state was held in Bali, Indonesia, in 1976, nearly 10 years after the founding of ASEAN. Before 1976, the key decision-making body was the annual meeting of ASEAN foreign ministers. During a summit, the heads of state of each of the ASEAN nations meet first to demonstrate the importance of ASEAN, set general directions for the body, and make long-term historic decisions. Meetings of ministers, or top government officials, from each country follow. The ministerial meetings involve reports on progress on previous decisions and may lay the groundwork for new directions. At the 1992 Fourth ASEAN Summit, for example, heads of state approved the ASEAN Free Trade Area, a major long-term decision to remove tariffs and increase free trade among member countries significantly affecting the economic future of the region.

There is no set schedule for ASEAN summits, but they have become more regular. Since 1976, there have been a total of 12 formal summits and four informal summits. All ASEAN countries except Myanmar have hosted a summit. Countries hosting summits rotate alphabetically. Given the alphabetical rotation system, the Twelfth ASEAN Summit should have been hosted by Myanmar, but instead it was held in the Philippines due to Myanmar's poor record on human rights and the possibility of boycotts by various countries. Singapore hosted the Thirteenth ASEAN Summit, celebrating the fortieth anniversary of ASEAN, in November 2007. There, heads of state approved a new ASEAN charter.

MINISTERIAL MEETINGS

The meetings of foreign ministers and economics and finance ministers are still key to the work of ASEAN. Economics and finance ministers began meeting after the UN issued a report recommending that they do so as ASEAN became more involved in economic affairs. Ministers from 10 member countries meet in five fixed, or permanent, economic committees, three noneconomic and rotating committees, and seven ASEAN committees with dialogue countries and international organizations.

Malaysian Prime Minister Abdullah Ahmad Badawi *(center)* leads an ASEAN meeting of economic ministers. In order to meet one of ASEAN's goals to stabilize the regional economy, the members have formed several economic committees that include finance ministers from each of their governments. In these committees, officials draft guidelines for new projects and initiatives and also organize new activities.

Once the foreign ministers or other ministers decide on something, a standing committee takes the decision further. The ongoing work of ASEAN is carried out by the standing committee. The standing committee is comprised of five individuals, the foreign minister of the host country, and the four resident ambassadors of the ASEAN countries. The committee meets several times each year. For example, if Singapore was scheduled to host the annual meeting of ASEAN foreign ministers, then its foreign minister would be the chairman of the standing committee, with the other four members being the Indonesian Ambassador to Singapore, the Malaysian Ambassador to Singapore, the Philippines Ambassador to Singapore, and the Thai Ambassador to Singapore. Each of the five countries has an ASEAN National Secretariat, which carries out the decisions made by the standing committee in its country. Under the standing committee are other ASEAN committees, some permanent and others more short-term.

THE SECRETARY-GENERAL AND THE SECRETARIAT

At the first summit in Bali, Indonesia, in 1976, leaders agreed to create an ASEAN secretary-general and a permanent central ASEAN secretariat in Jakarta, Indonesia. Prior to this, ASEAN had no central staff of its own and relied instead on national secretariats. Both of these changes made ASEAN a more centralized and stable organization, with a skilled staff that has a deep understanding of the organization. ASEAN foreign ministers appoint the secretary-general, the main person in charge of running the organization. The secretary-general comes from each country in ASEAN in turn, in order of the country's position in the alphabet, and serves for five years. The secretary-general runs the secretariat with the assistance of two deputies. The two deputies rotate among the ASEAN nations, each serving for five years.

The ASEAN secretariat is a permanent staff member for the organization, with a permanent office and headquarters. This secretariat opened in 1976 in Jakarta. Indonesia provides the land for the ASEAN secretariat—a seven-story building, local staff, and a car and house for the secretary-general. The annual budget for the ASEAN secretariat is US $8 million; each ASEAN member country, whether wealthy or poor, contributes an equal amount toward this budget. Countries' budgets and international grants cover the costs of many ASEAN meetings.[17]

At the central ASEAN secretariat in Jakarta there are 70 local staff and 40 professional staff. The local staff is largely Indonesian; they have jobs requiring fewer skills and earn less than the professionals. National governments nominate high-level staff for rotating positions, such as secretary-general and deputy secretary-general. The other professionals are recruited

Dr. Surin Pitsuwan (*above*) began his five-year term as secretary-general of ASEAN in 2008. The role of the secretary-general is to maintain cordial relations among the member nations, dialogue partners, and outside organizations. This encourages progress in economic and social initiatives, as well as security in the region.

internationally for their expertise and are paid high salaries. They are referred to as openly recruited international staff.

There are four basic functional units under the secretary-general. First, the economic cooperation unit works to improve and increase economic relations among the ASEAN nations. Much of its work has focused on the implementation of the ASEAN Free Trade Area (AFTA), which is an extremely complex process. Second, the functional cooperation unit works to foster relations in the social and cultural areas. A concrete example of work in this area is to encourage greater cooperation among the ASEAN nations in promoting the region as a tourist destination. In 1992, the general research unit became a unit focused on carrying out the ASEAN Free Trade

Agreement. This agreement says that eventually there should be no tariffs on imports or exports within the ASEAN region. The security cooperation unit is responsible for addressing the region's security concerns. Following 9/11, one of their major activities has been to coordinate ASEAN regional efforts against international terrorism.

At the secretariat, four professional directors are in charge of the four basic functional units, and eight assistant directors serve directly under them. There are 15 senior officers and other well-trained expert staff. Altogether there are about 40 professional staff members.

ASEAN national secretariats also continue to function in each country. Before the establishment of the ASEAN secretariat, national secretariats did most of the administrative work of the organization, and each had a national secretary-general. The director-generals of these national secretariats are senior officials from the respective Ministries of Foreign Affairs. Each is responsible for the ASEAN national secretariat in his or her country. Regular government officials—career civil servants, not politicians—from each country are reassigned to work for the ASEAN national secretariats. The major responsibility of these secretariats is to carry out ASEAN policies and activities in their respective countries and also to plan meetings scheduled for their country.

Much of the work of ASEAN is done in various annual meetings and other meetings that occur throughout the year. In 1993, there were about 100 meetings a year. By the year 2000 that number had increased to about 400 meetings a year. Currently there are about 600 ASEAN meetings each year. That contrasts with about 2500 meetings in the European Union.[18]

ASEAN and Cambodia

CAMBODIA IS THE NEWEST ASEAN MEMBER STATE, JOINING the regional organization in 1999. Since becoming an independent country in 1953, after a long period of trying to end French-colonial control and influence, Cambodia has been a country of great promise, a place of political instability, and a society of devastation and chaos. It was bombed and invaded, and it was the scene of a barbaric social experiment. ASEAN became actively involved in international diplomacy surrounding many of these complex events and problems, arguably making its first major entrance onto the world political stage.

During the 1960s, Cambodia's capital, Phnom Penh, was the most pleasant city in Southeast Asia, and Cambodia was an island of peace in a sea of conflict. Though it was economically poor, most of its people had plenty to eat and were quite content. In 1967, Prince Sihanouk, the royal leader of Cambodia, declined the invitation to join ASEAN. Sihanouk was a neutralist who wanted to keep Cambodia out of the Cold War and to side neither with the United States nor the Soviet Union. He also wanted to keep Cambodia out of the U.S. war in Vietnam. He thought Cambodia would inevitably be drawn into the Vietnam War and the U.S. sphere if Cambodia joined anti-Communist ASEAN.

As king of Cambodia in the 1940s and 1950s, Sihanouk had worked hard to free Cambodia from French rule, becoming a hero in the eyes of his people. He was especially popular in rural parts of Cambodia, to which he made frequent visits. But many urban professionals felt he ignored and neglected them and refused to bring them into power in a constitutional monarchy that included a parliament.

The United States mistrusted Sihanouk because he remained neutral in the Cold War. The United States saw him as being soft on Communism and accused him of looking the other way when Vietnamese Communists used his territory to strike against South Vietnam. Sihanouk, in turn, accused the United States of violating Cambodian airspace when, in March 1969, the United States began the secret bombing of what it claimed were Communist military bases in Cambodia, near the Vietnamese border.[19] This bombing lasted until 1973; at one stage, there were 80 B-52s dropping bombs on the Cambodian countryside daily.

U.S. President Richard Nixon and Secretary of State Henry Kissinger supplemented the bombings by sending U.S. troops into Cambodia to root out the Communists. U.S. policymakers knew that Sihanouk would never allow this, so in March 1970, while Sihanouk was traveling abroad, General Lon Nol and other Cambodian politicians overthrew Sihanouk, allegedly with the support of the United States. A few months later, the United States, with General Lon Nol's approval, invaded Cambodia, setting off a wave of protests in the United States. At Kent State University in Ohio, police killed four students and wounded nine others who were peacefully protesting the invasion.

After the overthrow of Sihanouk in March 1970, the country, renamed the Khmer Republic, endured five years of bloody civil war between Lon Nol and the Khmer Rouge (Red Khmer), the Cambodian Communists. Primarily because of Sihanouk's popularity in the countryside, the Khmer Rouge was extremely weak during his rule. But after his overthrow, a very bitter Prince Sihanouk lent his prestige and name to the Communist Khmer Rouge, greatly strengthening them in the countryside.

When the United States began to remove support for Lon Nol as part of its military withdrawal from Southeast Asia, his government was doomed, and the Khmer Rouge took control on April 17, 1975. Cambodia became a new Communist state called Democratic Kampuchea (DK). With refugees fleeing bombings and fighting in the countryside prior to the Khmer Rouge takeover, Phnom Penh had grown to a huge city of nearly two million. After the Khmer Rouge victory, virtually all the people of Phnom Penh were marched back to the countryside to become farmers. The next three years saw an intense social experiment to create an extreme barbaric form of Communism. Nearly two million people died in the process in an era known as the Killing Fields. The 1984 Academy Award–nominated film, *The Killing Fields*, based on the true story of the *New York Times* Pulitzer Prize–winning journalist, Sydney Schanberg, vividly shows how U.S. bombings devastated the Cambodian countryside and killed many innocent people, including women and children. Many villages were destroyed by mistake.

During the brutal Khmer Rouge regime people largely died of starvation, overwork, and poor health conditions, though some were tortured and executed because of their prior support of the Lon Nol regime and the Americans or because they resisted the new rulers. Many better-educated Cambodians, politicians, writers, scientists, and artists were killed, but some survived and are now active professionally or politically in or outside of Cambodia.

Many wonder how the gentle Buddhist Khmers of the peaceful Cambodia of the 1960s could have become so barbaric

When the Khmer Rouge emerged victorious in the Cambodian civil war, their leader Pol Pot ordered all citizens back to the countryside to work in the fields. Millions of people were executed, tortured, or simply starved and worked to death in the fields *(above)*. It is estimated that Cambodia lost 30 percent of its population during this time.

under the Khmer Rouge. There are two possible explanations: first, the Khmer Rouge was not the same everywhere, and in some areas they may not have engaged in such barbaric actions (in fact, without a modern system of communication, it would have been difficult to enforce the exact same system throughout the country); second, the intense bombing of the Khmer countryside with so much death and destruction created extreme bitterness against the system that produced those bombs—that is, the Lon Nol regime and the Americans who worked closely with it. Death became an everyday occurrence. The U.S. bombing was a terrible form of human abuse. As is common in child abuse, those who have been horribly abused can in turn become terrible abusers. This may explain why many of the Khmer Rouge became so barbaric.

THE VIETNAMESE INVASION (OR INTERVENTION)

On December 25, 1978, Vietnamese troops invaded Cambodia in a quick blitzkrieg attack.[20] From the Vietnamese perspective, this was an intervention, not an invasion. By mid-January they had seized Phnom Penh and driven the Khmer Rouge to the western countryside. They installed a more moderate, pro-Vietnamese, pro-Soviet, Communist government, the People's Republic of Kampuchea (PRK), and the country returned to normalcy. In subsequent months and years, Vietnamese forces were engaged in fighting the Khmer Rouge forces primarily in the western areas of the country, near the Thai border. Many Cambodians fled to Thailand as refugees to avoid the conflict. In fact, the Khmer refugee camps along the border became Cambodia's "second-largest city."[21] The most famous camp was Khao-I-Dang, which existed from 1979 to 1992. In mid-1983 there were about 57,500 refugees living there. Its residents were considered formal refugees, eligible for resettlement in countries like the United States and Canada. As they pursued the Khmer Rouge soldiers, the Vietnamese troops sometimes violated the Thai border. Thailand, to protect itself, planted many land mines in the areas bordering Cambodia. Even today, Thais face the threat of injury or death from those land mines.

ASEAN REACTION

In its declaration, ASEAN pledged a commitment to respect existing governments and their national sovereignty. Therefore, the expansion of Vietnamese Communism into Cambodia and the violation of Thai borders greatly alarmed ASEAN.

Many Southeast Asian leaders, as well as U.S. policymakers, believed in the domino theory. This was an idea held by U.S. policymakers that if one country became Communist, other neighboring countries would follow. It was first used in the 1950s to talk about threats to Southeast Asia after the Chinese Communists came to power in 1949 and Communist North Korea invaded South Korea. Events of 1975 supported the domino theory. Cambodia became Communist on April 17, Vietnam on April 30, and Laos on December 2, all in the same year.

The Vietnamese invasion of Cambodia represented conflict between two Communist countries and resulted in one Communist government replacing another. Thus, this was basically a conflict between nation-states, not between Communists and anti-Communists. However, a Communist Cambodia dominated by the Vietnamese was seen as militarily much more powerful and dangerous than the previous low-technology Khmer Rouge regime, which was focusing on changing society inside its own borders. Vietnam had the world's third-largest army, confident and seasoned after having defeated two major Western powers—France and the United States. Thus, Cambodia became a much more dangerous domino after the Vietnam invasion. Even though the invasion had removed a barbarous regime from power, the ASEAN consensus was to oppose Vietnam's 1978 invasion of Cambodia.

If Thailand, the country that bordered Cambodia and into which some Vietnamese troops had gone, were to become Communist, then the next dominos could be Malaysia, Burma, and Singapore. In 1976, Vietnam had expressed support for revolutionary movements throughout Southeast Asia. Thailand had an active insurgency in its poorest, most disadvantageous northeastern region. Thailand felt immediately threatened.

The Vietnamese invasion fundamentally violated the basic preamble of the ASEAN Declaration that does not allow for any "external interference in any form" and guarantees each nation's sovereignty. They also violated the principle that military force should not be used as a means to resolve political disputes.[22]

ASEAN, in a unified diplomatic position, opposed the Vietnamese-backed Cambodian government and lobbied successfully against its having a seat in the UN. In 1979, by a vote of 91–21, the UN approved a resolution calling for an end to the conflict, the withdrawal of Vietnamese forces, and an international conference.[23] Most of the votes in support of Vietnam were from the Soviet bloc. China, although it is a Communist nation, strongly supported the ASEAN position and had provided military support to the Khmer Rouge in their fight against the Vietnamese.

ASEAN also campaigned to block international economic aid needed to rebuild Cambodia's war-torn economy. The United States had responded to the invasion by stopping all U.S. economic trade with Vietnam. The United States was also active in blocking Vietnam from getting aid from international organizations. This was relatively easy since the United States dominated organizations such as the World Bank and the International Monetary Fund (IMF).

ASEAN subsequently lobbied effectively to convene an International Conference on Kampuchea (ICK), which took place in July 1981 in New York City. Ninety-two countries joined the conference. The Soviet Union and its allies, Vietnam and Laos, refused to participate. Even though the conference was not able to change the Cambodian government immediately, it helped create a strong opposition movement with support to its claim of being the legitimate government of Cambodia, and continued to press for change. In July 1982, three groups—the Khmer Rouge, Prince Sihanouk's Armée Nationale Sihanoukiste (ANS), and the Khmer People's National Liberation Front (KPNLF)—came together as the Coalition Government of Democratic Kampuchea (CGDK). ASEAN successfully lobbied the international community to give a UN seat to this group, making it the "legitimate" government of Cambodia, even though it controlled less than 20 percent of the country.

VIETNAM WITHDRAWS TROOPS

In the 1980s, as Vietnam still struggled to control Cambodia (called People's Republic of Kampuchea, or PRK, during the

(continues on page 74)

CAMBODIA'S
NORODOM SIHANOUK (1922–)

Norodom Sihanouk of Cambodia in the 1970s was at the center of Cold War conflicts and terrible turmoil in Southeast Asia. In 2006, he was in the news again when he demanded that the bones of the Khmer Rouge victims be cremated according to Buddhist tradition, rather than kept as evidence of an unimaginable political brutality and as a tourist attraction. The bones are on display at the Cheung Ek killing fields, managed by a Japanese private company. Each month several thousand tourists flock to a Buddhist shrine containing victims' skulls; also on view are the pits from which the bodies were recovered. The prosecution of the Khmer leaders, now in their 70s and 80s, is underway, though Sihanouk has said the trials will be ineffective.

Sihanouk was the son of King Norodom Suramarit and Queen Sisowath Kossamak of Cambodia. Sihanouk became king of Cambodia in 1941, when Cambodia was still a French colony. Like many leaders in the 1950s in the areas of Cambodia, Laos, and Vietnam, he demanded that the French grant Cambodia its independence. When Cambodia became independent in 1953, he returned from exile in Thailand.

During the Vietnam War, Sihanouk claimed he was trying to preserve Cambodia's neutrality. He ignored China's and North Vietnam's actions to base forces in Cambodia. China in turn bought Cambodian rice at high prices. As head of state and prince, he declined the invitation for Cambodia to become part of ASEAN. He had also opposed joining the earlier SEATO alliance. While Sihanouk was out of the country in March 1970, General Lon Nol, with alleged support by the United States, led a coup and overthrew him. Sihanouk explained his anger in his book, *My War with the CIA*, published in 1973. He fled to Beijing, China, and supported the Khmer Rouge (literally "Red Khmer," who were

Proud parents King Sihanouk and Queen Norodom *(center and left)* **greet the public with their son, Norodom Sihamoni, the new Cambodian king. Cambodians have enormous respect for their royal family, and they welcomed the family warmly when King Sihamoni returned to his homeland to take the throne.**

Communists) in their fight against Lon Nol. Sihanouk's popularity in the countryside of Cambodia increased the appeal of the Khmer Rouge.

When Cambodia was taken over by the Khmer Rouge, Sihanouk became the symbolic head of state again. He later spoke for the Khmer Rouge against the Vietnamese forces that invaded. He became head of a group of anti-Vietnamese forces, including his own political party and the Khmer Rouge, which was recognized

(continues)

(continued)

by the UN and supported by ASEAN. Vietnamese troops eventually withdrew in 1989 and with a transitional government overseen by the UN, Cambodia returned to a constitutional monarchy with Sihanouk as king. In 1999, during his reign, Cambodia became a formal member of ASEAN. Cambodia now has a multiparty democracy and a free market economy, as well as a symbolic monarch.

Since 1993 Sihanouk has been in ill health. He decided to abdicate, or leave his position, in 2004. Sihanouk is now called "king-father" and his son, Norodom Sihamoni, educated in music and dance in the former Czechoslovakia, succeeded him as Cambodia's new king.

(continued from page 71)

Vietnamese occupation), Vietnam aspired to the kind of economic success enjoyed by richer ASEAN countries. In 1986, it introduced *đôi mói*, or economic renovation, to make its economy more reliant on private property and market forces. With the collapse of the Soviet Union, Vietnam realized that it would need to rely on external assistance and trade from other countries, including the United States and those in the region. In 1988, Vietnam accelerated its withdrawal of troops from Cambodia, and in April 1989, Vietnam agreed to withdraw all of them. This decision opened the way for a resolution to the Cambodian problem and for Vietnam to have a new relationship with the ASEAN countries that previously had opposed it.

With the full withdrawal of Vietnamese forces, the 1991 Paris Conference on Cambodia called for by ASEAN resulted in accords that resolved the Cambodian question. The out-come reflected ASEAN's approach, though it would have preferred a transition without UN involvement. There would be two years of a UN-supervised transitional government under a supreme national council headed by Prince Sihanouk. Multiparty elections would follow in 1993, putting Cambodia on the path to Western-style democracy. After the withdrawal of Vietnamese troops and the transitional UN administration, Cambodia returned to its pre-1970 status as a constitutional monarchy with Sihanouk returning as king. Cambodia now has a multiparty democracy and recently had largely suc-cessful and fair nationwide local elections. Its free market economy is growing rapidly.

SUCCESS ON THE GLOBAL STAGE

With its highly successful international diplomacy on the Cambodian question leading to the eventual withdrawal of Vietnamese troops, ASEAN clearly graduated to a new, more mature level as a regional organization. ASEAN was consid-ered a major success story in the political and security arena. Scholars David Jones and M.L.R. Smith described this ASEAN political success at the global level as follows:

> ASEAN's success in mobilizing the international com-munity against Vietnamese rule in Kampuchea signaled its apparent arrival as a mature regional organization, marking the [A]ssociation's passage from an inchoate and vulnerable collection of states to effective inter-national partnership with a growing impact on the regional security order.[24]

On the other hand, Cold War developments led in the same direction that ASEAN was trying to go. The Soviet Union, which had supported Vietnam, and China, which had supported the Khmer Rouge, began to move closer together in their foreign policies in the mid-1980s. Then, in the late 1980s, the Soviet Union, which had supported Vietnam, collapsed. Vietnam's loss of its major international supporter certainly influenced its change in policies toward Cambodia. The United States and Australia offered as a compromise the idea of an interim UN transitional government, which was opposed by ASEAN.[25]

Nevertheless, as a result of its work in resolving the Cambodian question, ASEAN became a serious and visible player in the international arena and moved onto the world stage for the first time.

The Creation of a Free Trade Area: A Second Success Story

IN THE 1990S, WITH THE GROWING ECONOMIC INFLUENCE OF Japan, the rise in power of China and India, and the Asian economic crisis of 1997, ASEAN shifted its focus to cooperation in the economic and finance areas. ASEAN made substantial advances toward becoming a free trade area, a region in which there are no tariffs or other trade barriers between the countries of the regional group. With its goal of creating an ASEAN Economic Community (AEC) by the year 2015, ASEAN is also eager to create both a customs union, an area with a single set of tariffs for imports from outside the region, and a single common market, an area with freedoms of movement for goods, wealth, and services.

The idea behind free trade is that lowering tariffs and other barriers in the region will allow manufacturers to become more efficient and competitive. Without tariff protection for some industries, only the best companies and products will win in the marketplace. Also, with a larger market encompassing the entire region, international investors will be attracted to the region because their products will be able to reach a bigger market.

THE IDEA FOR AFTA

Singapore was first to suggest that ASEAN become a free trade area. It is logical that Singapore would initiate this idea. With only 4.4 million residents, it has the second-smallest home market in Southeast Asia, but its economy is the most advanced in the region. Singapore is, by far, the most international of all the Southeast Asian economies. Thus, the Southeast Asia region represents a potentially excellent market for Singaporean goods and services.

After Singapore proposed this idea, Thailand's prime minister, Anand Panyarachun, played a critical role in having it approved. As a former diplomat, he was well suited to convincing the six ASEAN members at the time to support the idea. Thailand was also a relatively prosperous and open economy. The ASEAN Free Trade Area, or AFTA, was formally approved at the Fourth ASEAN Summit in Singapore on January 28, 1992. The approved policy is known formally as the Agreement on the Common Effective Preferential Tariff (CEPT) Scheme for the ASEAN Free Trade Area.

THE CEPT AGREEMENT

There are many important elements to the CEPT Agreement. In this age of interdependent economies, many factories in different locations may contribute to final goods (goods purchased by the end user rather than used in the production of another good). A car that comes off an assembly line (perhaps in the United States) is a final good. Its engine parts and brakes, which may have been made in Mexico; its electronic window controls, made in Thailand; and its carburetors, fuel pumps, and glass, made in China, are not final goods. So one key question the agreement tries to answer is, what counts as a good produced within ASEAN and thus is subject to the free trade agreement? A manufactured product is considered ASEAN-produced if at least 40 percent of its content comes from a member nation. For example, if 50 percent of a Thai pickup truck is made in Thailand, then it is considered an ASEAN product.

The agreement provides for gradual tariff (import tax) reductions for all manufactured products (for example, a refrigerator); capital goods (for example, machinery used to produce auto engines); and processed agricultural products (for example, tapioca pudding made from the cassava plant or canned baby corn). The first goal is to have no tariffs above 20 percent after five to eight years. Then, within the next seven years, tariffs are to be reduced below 20 percent in amounts of 5 percent.

All quantitative restrictions or quotas on products moving between ASEAN countries are to be eliminated. So, for example, Thailand cannot limit the number of imported Malaysian cars. Member states will remove other nontariff barriers, such as those affecting sale of pharmaceuticals, on a gradual basis within five years.

Some products are regarded as highly sensitive or general exceptions and are not covered by these rules. Rice, for example, is on the highly sensitive list, because it is a crucial export-earner for both Thailand and Vietnam. They are two of the world's top three rice exporters. Other unprocessed agricultural goods are not excluded. General exceptions to the agreement include articles of artistic, historic, or archaeological value. Art dealers from Thailand, for example, would not be able to import artistic treasures from Angkor Wat in Cambodia. Items related to public morals, such as pornographic magazines, are not part of the agreement. Because the

A free trade zone established in Southeast Asia has been a crucial factor in encouraging economic development and stability. While most items do not have any taxes or tariffs imposed on them, other exported goods, like rice, may be taxed due to their importance to a country's income.

ASEAN countries are at different stages of development, the newer members such as Cambodia, Myanmar, Laos, and Vietnam have been given more time to reduce and eliminate tariffs under a modified schedule.

ASEAN is trying to move faster in some economic areas. It is focusing on reducing tariffs on information and communications technology equipment, electronics, textiles and clothing, agricultural processing, rubber-based products, cars and car parts, health care, fisheries, and wood-based products.

CARS, MALAYSIA, AND FREE TRADE IN ASEAN

In 2007, Malaysia's national carmaker, Proton, launched three new models at the Thailand Auto Expo. It had recently launched new car models in Singapore, Brunei, and Indonesia. These four ASEAN countries have become extremely important to Proton's car sales. Proton has also concluded a partnership with a Chinese company, and is hoping to sell to the growing Chinese market for cars. For a while, Proton was considering merging with another large car company like Germany's Volkswagen AG or the United States' General Motors. In 2007, it was also thinking about teaming up with carmakers in Iran and Turkey to create a special "Islamic car," which would have features like a compass pointing to Mecca and a special compartment to keep a copy of the Koran and a headscarf. At the same time, Proton is trying to hold on to the car market in Malaysia, where internationally made cars are increasingly popular.*

Through research into new technology and more efficient production processes, Proton is trying to stay competitive in the regional and global car markets. Forty-five minutes from Kuala Lumpur, Malaysia's capital, Proton is building Malaysia's first "auto city," a gigantic car plant called Tanjung Malem. It would cover 1,280 acres, have the capacity to produce one million cars per year, and workers would try to make attractive cars with lower costs.

Proton, which stands for Perusahaan Otomobil Nasional (National Automobile Enterprise), was founded in 1983 under the direction of Malaysia's prime minister, Tun Mahathir Mohamad. At that time, Malaysia was primarily an agricultural country, with an income based on rubber, palm oil, and tin. Some oil also had been discovered in the South China Sea. But the Malaysian government was determined to industrialize the country, making Malaysia less

(continues)

(continued)

dependent on other countries for industrial goods. Malaysia supported Proton by creating very high import taxes—up to 300
percent—on cars made in other countries, giving Proton a great
advantage and making it the dominant car in Malaysia. Proton
thrived, though many in the auto industry said the quality of
the car was not very high. Companies making automobile parts
became more prevalent. The Japanese car company Mitsubishi
shared some of its technology and trained Proton staff. Proton was
not just a car company, but also an important part of Malaysia's
effort to become a modern, industrial country.

In January 1992, at the Fourth ASEAN Summit in Singapore,
the ASEAN heads of government agreed to establish an ASEAN
free trade area. ASEAN's free trade agreement, CEPTA, together
with new international trade rules, called this strategy into question. The agreement meant that Malaysia had to lower tariffs on
cars produced in other ASEAN countries. Trade conflicts broke out
between Malaysia and Thailand, a large car market and carmaker
itself. Malaysia refused to cut its import taxes on cars and car parts
made in Thailand. Thailand put high tariffs on palm oil imports from
Malaysia. Malaysia negotiated a delay on reducing its car tariffs
to between 0 percent and 5 percent until 2005. Now the tariffs
must be below 5 percent by 2008. In the new competitive ASEAN
regional and world market, Proton has been struggling to keep up.[**]

---

[*] "Ailing Proton Looks to Mecca," *Asia Sentinel*, December 8, 2007.
Available online at *http://www.asiasentinel.com*.

[**] Tamar Gabilaia, "Malaysian Proton and AFTA: Threat or Advantage?", TED
Case Studies, June 2001. Available online at *http://www.american.edu/TED.
proton.htm*; Chee Yoke Heong, "Malaysia's Proton Struggles On," *Asia Times*,
2003. Available online at *http://www.atimes.com*.

GOING BEYOND FREE TRADE TO AN ECONOMIC COMMUNITY (AEC)

In 2003, ASEAN declared the goal of attaining an ASEAN Economic Community (AEC) by 2020. In January 2007, they moved the target year forward to 2015. The goal is to move to a greater level of economic cooperation, beyond mere free trade to ASEAN as a single common market with a free flow of goods, services, business investments, and wealth. This vision includes an emphasis on wider-spread economic development and a reduction of poverty and socioeconomic inequalities in the region. Unfortunately, ASEAN does not have the funds to address serious inequalities among countries of the region or within the countries.

In January 2007, ASEAN leaders signed an agreement about workers who migrate across borders. The agreement asks each government to draw up a list of rights to which migrant workers are entitled, such as due process of the law and basic services such as health care and education. Many workers in the region are on the move, legally and illegally. The Philippines, Indonesia, Myanmar, Cambodia, Vietnam, and Laos export workers; Singapore and Brunei import labor; and Thailand and Malaysia do both.

ASEAN'S ECONOMIC SUCCESS

Economists say that there has been a dramatic increase in international companies coming to ASEAN countries but that the ASEAN market needs to become even bigger to succeed.[26] Singapore and Malaysia, among the wealthiest ASEAN countries with the most buying power and best communications and transportation, have benefited most.

All ASEAN nations, especially Vietnam, Cambodia, Singapore, and the Philippines, have shown significant increases in their real income per capita, and this may be partly related to freer trade. But there are still dramatic differences in average per person income in the region. Singapore's income per capita is 28 times higher than that of Myanmar. Thailand's income per capita is four times that of the Lao PDR. Some of the poorest countries, such as Cambodia, Laos, Myanmar, and Vietnam, depend on tariffs rather than taxes on their own people to fund their basic services.[27] Because these countries are relatively poor with small economies, their businesses do not yield many taxes. Rich countries such as Singapore do not need such import taxes.

There are also companies, regions, communities, workers, and families that "win," or do better than before, as a result of free trade. Other companies, regions, workers, and families "lose" income and opportunities in the new economic competition unleashed by freer trade. As a result of free trade, for example, some Indonesian companies and their factory workers producing Nike shoes have lost out to Vietnamese companies, which can make the same shoes less expensively. Cassava, the plant that gives us tapioca, is common in northeast Thailand. As a result of freer trade between the EU and Africa, the European market for Thai cassava has declined. Many cassava growers in Northeast Thailand have lost livelihoods. Currently, however, with freer trade in oil, cassava is being promoted as a renewable energy source to be mixed with oil to produce less-polluting gasoline for vehicles. Thus, the Thai cassava losers may become winners, and the world may also gain from the use of cassava, as it will slow down global warming.

Some researchers are skeptical about the benefits of free trade areas, and ASEAN's AFTA in particular. They point out that trade within ASEAN has not grown very much, at least not much more than trade with other countries. They say that excluding rice from free trade means that significant trade barriers exist. It also may be that the well-being of a country and its population is tied to the ability to protect some local industries or agriculture from regional competition or that the income from tariffs is important for the country to be able to fund

While free trade may have many benefits for regional economic development, sometimes it can harm as well as help. When the European Union approved of free trade between their organization and Africa, the demand for Thai cassava dropped sharply. Thai cassava harvesters (*above*) lost their only source of income in the deal.

some basic services.[28] Further investment in human resource development may be more important than free trade.

Other scholars and many businessmen see the movement toward free trade areas as extremely positive. Those hoping for an Asian Renaissance argue that regional integration has helped the Asian economies.[29] They say that East Asian economies need to push aggressively for regional cooperation as a way to achieve economies of scale (improving efficiency and productivity by having extremely large markets and many large companies) through appropriate specialization. One journalist writing about globalization describes his travels through the Mekong Delta in South Vietnam, observing Vietnamese rice farmers who have benefited from the elimination of trade barriers and who now enjoy a standard of living unimaginable only a few years ago.[30] These farmers are the direct beneficiaries of Vietnam's economic renovation policy and its integration into the ASEAN and global economy. Vietnam now has one of the fastest-growing economies in the world.

Many trade barriers within the ASEAN region have been reduced or eliminated. There also seems to be a clear commitment to move toward achieving ASEAN's goal of an economic community by the year 2015. In this sense, AFTA represents a second major accomplishment of ASEAN, following its first important accomplishment in helping resolve the complex situation in Cambodia in the 1970s, 1980s, and 1990s.

ASEAN Programs and Activities

In 2006, ASEAN COUNTRIES ATTRACTED 56.4 MILLION VISITORS from all over the world.[31] ASEAN encourages tourism because it is a major source of income for Southeast Asians and a boost to the economy. ASEAN also developed a tourism Web site that they've named ASEAN: Asia's Perfect 10 Paradise. This site highlights the 10 countries that make up ASEAN and promotes it as a great place to meet friendly people, experience year-round warm temperatures, and enjoy beautiful beaches and cultures at relatively low costs.

Citizens of ASEAN countries can travel for up to two weeks to ASEAN countries without a visa; all the person needs is a passport. In a recent survey of citizens of the region, 49.3 percent indicated that they had visited another ASEAN country.[32]

(continues on page 90)

SEEING THE WORLD'S HERITAGE IN SOUTHEAST ASIA: ANGKOR WAT

Regarded as the supreme masterpiece of Khmer architecture and the largest religious monument in the world, Angkor Wat is a huge temple built between 1113 and 1150 in what is today the country of Cambodia. It is surrounded by a moat 570 feet wide and 4 miles long. It is built out of sandstone and laterite, in the architecture characteristic of its time and is influenced by the Hindu and Buddhist religions. On the inner wall of the moat is the world's longest bas-relief in the world, once painted and gilded. Bas-relief is a method of carving stone—the design is etched into the stone with the main figures higher than the background, so that the sculpture is more like a painting than a statue. In the area around Angkor Wat, spreading out over about 41 miles (67 square kilometers), are many other temples built between the eighth and thirteenth centuries. This region was the capital city of the ancient Khmer Empire. Recent research published by the National Academy of Sciences (August 2007), using both ground surveys and aerial scans, confirm that Angkor at that time was the center of an "incredibly vast city with an elaborate water network." The city had some of the "most complicated hydraulic works the world had ever seen."

Angkor Wat is one of the most popular tourist destinations in the ASEAN countries. In 1993, the United Nations Economic, Scientific and Cultural Organization (UNESCO) designated it a protected World Heritage Site, an outstanding cultural or natural site that is an important part of the common heritage of humanity.

About a million people visit this area each year, many traveling to various temples in the 41-mile area. The Cambodian government has to balance its need for tourist revenue with concerns about preserving the site. "The ancients built the temples for religious purposes, not for such crowds of tourists to climb on," said Khun Sokha, a tour guide there. "The harm is obvious. We are worried, but the people's livelihood depends on these tourists."* Southeast

The temples of Angkor Wat *(above)* have provided Cambodia with a steady source of income via the tourism industry. Declared a UNESCO World Heritage Site, Angkor Wat's surge in popularity has become a danger to itself, as the Cambodian government is reluctant to limit access to its most profitable asset.

Asia has other famous world heritage sites: Ayutthaya, the ancient capital of Thailand with unique Buddhist architecture; Bali, the Hindu-oriented island of Indonesia noted for its beaches and arts and crafts; Borobudur, a group of ancient Buddhist monuments on the island of Java in the archipelago of Indonesia; and Halong Bay, a huge bay of 2,000 limestone islands off the north coast of Vietnam.

* "Angkor Wat facing a 500-year-old problem," *Taipei Times*, March 26, 2007. Available online at *http://www.taipeitimes.com/News/world/archives/2007/03/26/2003353917*).

(continued from page 87)

Travel within ASEAN countries is becoming easier. Now it is possible to travel by land among Vietnam, Laos, Cambodia, Thailand, and China. Railroads and highways are being constructed and maintained. In December 2006, a third bridge across the Mekong River was opened, linking Thailand and Laos. A $44-billion Asian highway network is a cooperative project among countries in Asia and the United Nations Economic and Social Commission for Asia and the Pacific (ESCAP). After several suspensions since 1959 due to wars and other issues, a major highway network totaling nearly 87,500 miles (140,000 kilometers) is finally nearing completion. The completed sections of the corridor have gone from being little more than dirt tracks just a few years ago to two-lane roads with concrete shoulders, drainage, and concrete bridges. The highway is aimed to link the economies of China, Myanmar, Laos, Vietnam, Thailand, and Cambodia.

ASEAN's railway system is also on the road to improvement. A train link between Kunming in southern China and Singapore is being constructed. Air travelers are also finding it easier to fly within the ASEAN region, as new airlines, such as Bangkok Airways and Air Asia, offer cheap flights between countries.

PROBLEMS WITH TOURISM

Although ASEAN promotes tourism in the region, the organization has been criticized for not addressing and—even contributing to—some of the problems increased tourism creates. Cambodia and Thailand in particular have become focal points for "sex tourism." Sex tourism is a kind of travel organized by businesses that allows men to have short-term sexual relations with prostitutes at travel destinations. The United Nations and many other groups are trying to eliminate sex tourism because it is dangerous and encourages the powerful and wealthy to violate the dignity of poor women and sometimes even children.

This has become a huge problem that is difficult to prevent. For example, since ASEAN countries no longer require visas from their residents, it has become easier for Vietnamese women to migrate to Cambodia in order to work in the commercial sex industry. As tourists they are not supposed to work, but such laws in Cambodia are not actively enforced. Thousands of Burmese girls have migrated to northern Thailand, where 70 percent to 80 percent of tourists are men, and some of these girls have been enticed to work in the sex industry.[33] In fact, sex tourism in Southeast Asia (particularly in Thailand and Cambodia) is openly promoted on the Internet in Europe and East Asia. Since tourism makes up about 8 percent of the Thai economy, the Thai government allows the commercial sex industry to flourish. Given ASEAN's declaration not to interfere in the domestic policies of member countries, other ASEAN countries refuse to criticize Thailand and Cambodia for tolerating an active commercial sex industry. Sex for money is also becoming a problem in Vietnam, and the Communist Party there is concerned about what they see as a growing "social evil."

Most of the women working in the sex industry are from remote, disadvantaged rural areas and have limited formal education. Many Thai women are divorced and are considered "used." They have limited remarriage prospects with local Thai men. It is not uncommon for unmarried and married Thai men to visit prostitutes.

Some women involved in the sex industry are virtually slaves in brothels. Others, working primarily in the international tourist sector, are independent agents and can make large amounts of money to help their families in poor, rural areas.

Within the ASEAN region, however, there is a movement to protect minors. Working closely with the United States, Sweden, and New Zealand, ASEAN countries have begun severely punishing adult sex with children. Recently, Thai police arrested a Canadian pedophile, Christopher Neil, who was sent back to

Canada to face charges and jail. A former deputy speaker of the Thai senate has been sentenced to 36 years in prison for having sex with minors. Two Thai teachers were recently sentenced to 50 years in jail for sexually molesting young girls. Globally, activists have become involved in this issue. New York attorney Guy Jacobson, after becoming aware of this problem while traveling in Cambodia, started the Redlight Children Campaign, a worldwide grassroots initiative aimed at causing awareness and protecting children from the sex trade industry.

Tourism can also be dangerous to the environment. Some environmentalists argue that the reason the devastating Indian Ocean tsunami of 2004 was such a disaster in certain places was because coastal areas had been cleared to make beach resorts like those in Phuket. Businessmen began to develop Ko Chang (Elephant Island), on the Pacific side of Thailand near Cambodia, as an alternative destination. Ko Samet, a Thai national park, has lost many of its natural qualities because of the huge influx of backpacking tourists. This once pristine island is now being bulldozed into hundreds of new resorts.

A third negative effect of tourism relates to culture. For example, areas of northern Thailand are marketed as the home to "exotic" hill peoples. Their cultures are being marketed for revenue. Also, some young women from these ethnic groups have been pulled into the sex industry.[34] The promotion of such groups to tourists has led to dramatic increases in materialism among the hill peoples, resulting in a change to their culture. Now it is increasingly difficult to find hill people communities untouched by the influx of outsiders.

THE ASEAN POPULATION PROGRAM (APP)

The ASEAN Population Program (APP) is coordinated by the ASEAN Population Coordination Unit (APCU). It has received funding from Australia, the United Nations Fund for Population Activities (UNFPA), and the Food and Agricultural Organization (FAO). Among its activities have been studies on health and family planning issues in the region, training for those working in population and development agencies, and exchange of personnel working on issues such as women in development and migration and rural development.

In the wealthy city-state of Singapore, only 1.06 children are born on average for each woman of childbearing age, far below replacement level. In marked contrast, in the poor country of Laos 4.68 children are born for every woman.[35] These different fertility rates are probably related to the degree of poverty and education of women and the population as a whole in these two places. Where women and families are poorer, they tend to have more children, who often represent another pair of hands to work and help support families; but many of these children may die. Where families are better able to support themselves, they have fewer children. In the Philippines, fertility rates are also high (at 3.5) because the Catholic Church opposes birth control. In Malaysia, the government encourages the Malay population, the ethnic majority that has special preferences, to have five children. Indonesia promotes two-child families through advertising leadership training and free distribution of birth control pills and condoms. The rate of population growth there has fallen from 3 percent to 1.2 percent.[36]

Most people working for the development of poorer countries see that a high fertility rate will hurt a country's chances for climbing out of poverty. When families have many children, it is hard for women to contribute to the work force; each child gets less attention and fewer resources, and increased pressure is put on the country's limited education and health resources.

In the 1960s, Thailand had a high fertility rate (the average Thai woman had more than seven children). It was predicted that if the trend continued, Thailand would no longer be able to export rice, a major source of income. Since then, Thailand has had remarkable success in reducing its fertility rate to 1.64 children per woman of childbearing age. Key to Thailand's

Mechai Viravaidya *(right)*, known in Thailand as the "condom king," with Peter Piot from UNAIDS, aggressively pushed for family planning and safe-sex practices when poverty and AIDS threatened the well-being of Thai people and the economy. His methods were so successful, Thailand was one of the few countries in the 1990s to have a decline in HIV infections and a considerable reduction in its fertility rate.

success was the leadership of politician and activist Mechai Viravaidya, also known as "the condom king."[37] A health economist from a wealthy family and the founder of the Population and Community Development Association, he used humor and unusual methods to focus the public's attention on public health and family planning. He emphasized that if family planning were to succeed, then health conditions had to be improved. If children are dying from poor health conditions, it becomes rational to have many children to ensure that some survive. After personally seeing how high fertility was contributing to poverty in remote, disadvantaged areas of Thailand, he realized that the advertising for family planning must be extremely aggressive. He promoted active awareness of condoms, even among children, and convinced people that the condom was a valuable, clean product that could be openly talked about.

Viravaidya's promotion of condom use increased safe-sex practices in a country with a notorious sex-trade industry that was believed to have set off an AIDS epidemic. First he had to force the government to admit that there was a serious AIDS problem. He also convinced them to have the police work with sex workers and drug addicts to reduce the spread of the HIV virus. Now Thailand boasts one of the lowest birthrates in Asia, and the spread of the HIV virus has slowed considerably. For his creative and dynamic efforts in promoting family planning and confronting the AIDS crisis, Viravaidya received the 1994 Ramon Magsaysay Award for Public Service, the Asian equivalent of the Nobel Prize.

LABOR PROGRAMS

In 1984, at a meeting of the ASEAN labor ministers, a decision was made to increase cooperation in the field of labor. One important rationale was to coordinate the position of ASEAN countries at international meetings of the International Labor Organization (ILO), a UN agency that works to improve labor conditions around the world. In addition, the ASEAN Program on Industrial Relations was initiated in order to have systems and practices that will contribute to "industrial peace, higher productivity, and social justice."[38] The ASEAN labor ministers

Due to their low production costs, countries like Vietnam make items for popular brands like Nike. Compared to American workers, these Vietnamese employees are paid a meager $59 a month, but in actuality, this amount is 14 percent higher than the national minimum wage. While stories of sweatshops and hard labor have been slightly exaggerated at times, ASEAN is concerned about workplace conditions in foreign corporations.

have met a total of 19 times and, in May 2000, in Manila, they issued a vision and mission statement.

A major recent concern has been the conditions of migrant workers. Some organizations claim that in the region there are many "sweatshops," or factories that treat their workers inhumanely—paying them very little, making them work under harsh and dangerous conditions, and requiring long hours. In 1999, the Workers' Rights Coalition strongly attacked Nike for having sweatshops in Southeast Asia, particularly in Vietnam. Nike initially responded that it did not actually make goods and that it was just buying shoes and apparel from Asian subcontractors who ran the factories. This is true, but it seemed like a lame excuse. As a result of the extensive criticisms, Nike began to monitor the labor conditions of its subcontractors more thoroughly. Vietnam also developed strict labor laws.

The issues raised by the Nike controversy are complex. One of the goals of ASEAN is to promote international investment in the region as a way to create needed job growth in the area. Countries such as Vietnam, Laos, and Cambodia actively pursue companies like Nike because they want all the jobs that will be created. Given huge differences in the cost of living between a country like Vietnam and the United States, it is unreasonable to compare wages in U.S. dollars. Also, given the extended family culture in Southeast Asia, workers often live together and pool their wages. Many of those working at factories producing Nike gear in Vietnam ride their bikes to work and enjoy highly subsidized lunches. Thus, what might seem to be a fair living wage in Vietnam may be far below what would be a fair living wage for workers in the United States, where living expenses are much higher. ASEAN is in a difficult position. It wants the jobs that come with international investments, but it also wants good working conditions for the people of the region.

DRUG AND NARCOTICS CONTROL

Northern Thailand, northeast Mynamar, and northwestern Laos are located in an area called the Golden Triangle, a source of drugs for the world market. The triangle refers to the shape of these three countries together, and gold probably refers to the gold that merchants used in earlier times to purchase the opium from which heroin is made. In the 1950s, and after the crackdown in Communist China on poppy growing and opium use, this mountainous area became a major supplier of heroin for the world market, with Burma as the leading supplier. Now methamphetamines also come from this area, especially from Myanmar. However, the UN reports that this area, which in the 1970s was producing more than 70 percent of the opium that was refined into heroin, is now producing only about 5 percent of the world's total.[39]

Efforts by ASEAN to fight the narcotics and drug trade in this area began in 1972. In 1976, ASEAN issued the Declaration of Principles to Combat the Abuse of Narcotic Drugs; it aims to have a drug-free ASEAN by 2015. ASEAN created four centers in Thailand, the Philippines, Malaysia, and Singapore to share information in their fight against the drug trade and to combat cross-border crime.

Thailand and Laos have also fought drug cultivation and the drug trade. The Thai royal family and the government have assisted the hill people, who traditionally grew opium poppies, to shift to alternative crops such as coffee, macadamia nuts, green vegetables, flowers, and strawberries. In Laos the government began a crackdown in the 1990s because they wanted to build their international reputation and because some Lao government officials were worried that their own children were being exposed to dangerous drugs. China pressured Myanmar to stop producing opium along the Chinese border. The Wa peoples who lived there banned opium cultivation and welcomed Chinese investment in rubber, sugarcane, tea, and casinos.[40] The UN has encouraged governments to support alternative livelihoods for former opium farmers.

DISASTER MANAGEMENT

Southeast Asia is a region exposed to many kinds of hazards. Flooding from the Mekong River and its tributaries is the predominant hazard in Cambodia, Lao PDR, and Vietnam during the monsoon season. Flooding is made worse by the clogging of lakes and streams with soil from eroding land, the deterioration of drainage and irrigation systems, and the cutting of forests. Typhoons and intense thunderstorms with high winds affect the Philippines and Vietnam. Changes in ocean temperatures sometimes create droughts in Indonesia, causing widespread forest fires. Indonesia and the Philippines are located in the Pacific Ocean's "Ring of Fire," which often experiences earthquakes and volcanic eruptions. These hazards can cause great loss of life and terrible displacement of poor people. In the 1990s, disasters in Indonesia and Vietnam set back economic development. Also, a devastating cyclone hit coastal Myanmar in 2008.

Good disaster management includes many things, such as incorporating knowledge of hazards into planning for economic development, population location, and farming activities. It also means developing early warning systems and disaster response plans involving trained responders and money set aside to help those affected. Local communities need to participate in planning, and many different levels of government must work together in cooperation with nongovernmental organizations such as the International Red Cross, Catholic Relief Services, or Islamic Relief.

In 1971 ASEAN established an experts group on disaster management, and activities have continued since. In early 2003, ASEAN created the ASEAN Committee on Disaster Management (ACDM) to build a region of disaster-resilient nations and safer communities. The ASEAN Regional Program on Disaster Management (ARPDM) provides a framework for cooperation up until 2010, with 29 activities and 5 key priority areas.

Only a year later, on December 26, 2004, the Indian Ocean tsunami struck. Within days of the disaster, ASEAN leaders met in Jakarta to draw up an action plan to deal with the effects of the tsunami. They established an ASEAN Humanitarian Assistance Center to mobilize civilian and military personnel to assist in relief operations; encouraged the UN to mobilize the international community to support humanitarian relief; requested that organizations such as the World Bank, Asian Development Bank, and the Islamic Development Bank provide funds for relief operations; and requested assistance for an effective early warning center on both the Indian and Pacific ocean areas of Southeast Asia.

THE BATTLE AGAINST SARS AND BIRD FLU

Severe Acute Respiratory Syndrome (SARS) is a new, contagious, and fast-spreading respiratory virus that struck Asia in late 2002 and early 2003. It originally broke out in China in November 2002, and then struck Hong Kong. In an age of international travel, it eventually spread all over the globe. Scientists believe, like many new viruses, it may have come from animals, perhaps the Asian palm civet (a cat-sized mammal with a face like a raccoon). Over 8,000 people developed SARS, and 774 died of the disease.

The crisis posed a threat not only to the people of China and Southeast Asia but also to the ASEAN tourism industry. Countries that usually sent many workers abroad found that their recruitment numbers of workers from other regions fell. For example, the Gulf countries temporarily stopped the entry of Filipino migrant workers. On April 26, 2003, the ASEAN leaders had met with the leaders of China, Japan, and Korea to discuss strategies for combating the SARS crisis. At the meeting an action plan was put into place, and ASEAN actively sought financial support from the UN's World Health Organization (WHO), ASEAN partners such as Japan and the United States, and other international agencies to eliminate SARS and its threat to the region. The ASEAN countries then worked together quickly to carry out the action plan to ensure that ASEAN would be free of SARS. Only two months later, ASEAN health ministers announced that the region was free of SARS, a major ASEAN success story.

In 2004, a new infectious disease emerged, the bird (or avian) flu. Migrating birds and waterfowl that are not harmed by it carry this virus. In the mid-1990s, it moved to chickens, which do get sick from it. That year dozens of people, mainly those who work on poultry farms in Thailand and Vietnam, were affected by it. Health experts worried that it would begin moving easily from person to person, like other kinds of flu, dwarfing the threat posed by SARS.

Outbreaks of bird flu in poultry are devastating to the economies of individual countries in Southeast Asia. Because of this, ASEAN has created a plan to respond to future incidents of avian flu. This plan includes an alarm system, vaccinations, and an information-sharing program among member countries.

In Thailand, chickens and ducks are often treated like pets. Cockfighting is an essential part of some village cultures. Poultry is a significant component of the Thai diet and was a major export, especially to Japan. When the disease broke out, Thai officials put their health system on high alert, immediately began cooperating with neighboring countries such as Cambodia, and worked with the WHO. Prime Minister Thaksin Shinawatra visited farmers and promised government compensation for the millions of chickens being killed to stamp out the bird flu before it spread further. Vietnam also paid for slaughtered animals. Indonesia reported that millions of its chickens were dying.[41]

By October 2005—by which time the bird flu had killed at least 65 people and many more animals in Cambodia, Thailand, Indonesia, and Vietnam—ASEAN ministers had developed a regional action plan to combat this deadly flu virus. The strategy laid out a three-year plan to create a surveillance and alert system to detect the disease, to provide vaccinations to eradicate the virus, and to develop emergency preparedness plans and information-sharing systems among countries. The ASEAN bloc urged the world to provide financial and technical support for the anti–bird flu task force, and has already received $2 million in promises of support.[42] In November 2007, the ASEAN ministers for agriculture and forestry continued to fight bird flu, while the United Nations Food and Agriculture Organization announced that the disease was widespread in Indonesia. Fifteen other countries (including Vietnam, Indonesia, and Thailand) reported 359 human cases of the disease.[43]

RURAL DEVELOPMENT AND POVERTY ERADICATION PROGRAMS

In normal times, when there are no natural disasters such as floods or extreme drought, much of rural Southeast Asia is characterized by "affluent subsistence." This means that, even though rural people might be poor in terms of cash available per person, they have adequate shelter and plenty of nutritious food. For example, Thailand imports the least amount of food because it has an abundant variety of fruits and vegetables. Several countries in ASEAN have been successful in recent decades in reducing poverty levels. A noteworthy example is Vietnam. However, the region's growing prosperity was abruptly interrupted in July 1997, with the Asian economic crisis that started in Thailand.

ASEAN's rural development and poverty reduction program was a response to the economic crisis and the related Hanoi Plan of Action. This plan was approved at the Sixth ASEAN Summit in Hanoi, December 15–16, 1998. It is the first of a series of plans of action to realize the ASEAN Vision 2020 articulated in December 1997.[44] ASEAN's primary role was to assist in seeking external funding to help the region get back on its feet. ASEAN created the Action Plan on Rural Development and Poverty Eradication supported by funds from the United Nations Development Program (UNDP). The UNDP provides assistance to countries with critical needs. On December 15, 1997, the ASEAN Foundation was established to address unequal economic development in the region. The foundation has provided $16 million for over 100 projects during the past decade.[45]

Since the countries experiencing the crisis already owed a lot of money to countries whose banks and finance companies had made excessive loans to them, they turned to the World Bank, the International Monetary Fund, Asian Development Bank, and the UN for help. The Australian government also worked with ASEAN to identify people that especially needed help and to assist with meeting their basic needs. Worst hit by the crisis were Thailand, Indonesia, and the Philippines. In Thailand many companies and factories were forced to close and workers were let go.

In the countries affected, people were able to make some income through what is called the informal economy, the part of the economy that is not organized by bigger economic units or regulated by governments, like selling food or other items on the street. The informal economy helped those individuals who lost their jobs. Others returned to the countryside to their extended families. A large number of government workers were not affected and were able to provide help to their extended families. The crisis served as a wake-up call to the region, and major reforms were put into place after the crisis. To help keep kids in school during the crisis, Thailand implemented the first public-subsidized loan scheme for high school students. It also passed a major education amendment that made 12 years of education free for all and nine years of education compulsory. The region quickly recovered from the crisis.

THE FUTURE: MOVING BEYOND SECURITY AND TRADE

Complementing its success in the security and free trade areas, ASEAN has promoted cooperation in other areas. Many of these areas reflect ASEAN's shift away from just national state security to human security and the ability of people to live safe, secure, and happy lives. Some initiatives in these arenas have attracted funding and aid from outside sources like the UN, Japan, and the United States. Social and cultural development will likely become even more prominent in ASEAN in the future.

ASEAN Links
with the World

THE MAJOR WAY IN WHICH ASEAN CONNECTS TO THE REST OF
the world is by a system called dialogue partnerships. With
dialogue partnerships ASEAN seeks ongoing discussions in
which it would enter as an equal partner, not an inferior. The
first partnership was an informal dialogue with the European
Economic Community (EEC) in 1972. In 1973, ASEAN began
discussions with neighboring countries in its geographic
area—that year with Japan, in 1974 with Australia, and in 1975
with New Zealand. In 1977, it began partnerships with Canada
and the United States. Dialogues followed with South Korea in
1991 and China, Russia, and India in 1996.

Through these partnerships, ASEAN seeks to attain three
primary goals. First, it wants to increase the development assistance its members receive. Development assistance is loans or

grants from specific countries or from global institutions like the World Bank that help countries build up their economy and society. Second, ASEAN tries to attract international business investments. For example, it has attracted the Swedish automotive company Volvo to the region. Finally, it seeks ways to find and expand markets where ASEAN-made goods and services can be sold. Nike, the world-famous sports company, buys many of its products, such as shoes and apparel from many factories in Southeast Asia.

ASEAN LINKS WITH THE EU

The European Union is Europe's free trade area and customs union as well as a political union with significant lawmaking powers. Many Southeast Asian countries have a long history with Europe, due to their former colonial ties. Today, ASEAN is a key partner for Europe.

ASEAN has two primary objectives in linking with the European community. It wants to keep European markets open to exports from ASEAN, and it seeks development assistance from Europe.[46] Numerous meetings take place between Europe and ASEAN, including special summits attended by both European and Asian heads of state. European countries are involved in many projects in ASEAN countries. For example, the EU played a major role in providing relief after the tsunami and supported the peace process between Aceh (Indonesia) rebels and the Indonesian state. The EU provides training and scholarships for ASEAN nationals. The EU provides assistance in the areas of environment, energy, intellectual property rights, and education. The EU also offers its extensive experience with regional integration and helps in strengthening ASEAN's institutional structure, including the ASEAN secretariat.

ASEAN LINKS WITH JAPAN

Japan is a natural partner for ASEAN because of its long and enduring historical links with the region, going back 600 years.

Merchant ships from the Ryukyu Islands (now Okinawa, a prefecture of Japan with a large U.S. military base) came to Southeast Asia from the kingdom of Okinawa. In later centuries Red Seal ships of the Japanese Tokugawa period sailed to the region. The Thai kingdom of Ayutthaya had an active Japanese military and merchant community led by Nagamasa Yamada. During World War II, the Japanese Imperial Army invaded the region to gain access to vital natural resources crucial for its war machine. Japan saw itself as helping to liberate countries such as the Philippines, Indonesia, Burma, and Vietnam from their colonizers and promised these countries independence. Thus, Japan has been active in the region for centuries.

In the early decades of ASEAN, Japan was the dominant economic partner, both in terms of trade and investment. The Fukuda Doctrine in 1977 promoted three basic principles: Japan would never again pose a military threat to the region; Japan would actively sponsor cultural and people-to-people exchanges with Southeast Asia; and Japan would provide economic and financial support for ASEAN.

In 1981 the ASEAN-Japan Center in Tokyo was established. The role of this center is to promote Japanese imports from, investments in, and tourism to the ASEAN region.

Japanese markets are becoming more open to goods from ASEAN nations. Starting in the late 1980s, the Japanese opened many factories in the ASEAN region. At one point a new Japanese factory was opening every three days in Thailand. Japan also channeled the equivalent of billions of dollars of development and technical assistance to ASEAN nations through the ASEAN-Japan Development Fund and the Japan-ASEAN Comprehensive Exchange Plan. It began training many people living in ASEAN countries with new skills.

Japan has become the world's major aid power,[47] and ASEAN has been a major recipient of Japanese assistance. About 19 percent of Japan's total assistance to individual countries goes to Southeast Asia.[48] In 2004 Japan supplied 39 percent of

Fuchigami Joukei, a Japanese tourism official from the ASEAN-Japan Center, conducts a seminar with Filipino tour guides. The ASEAN-Japan Center in Tokyo, Japan, was established to encourage trade, tourism, and investment relations between the two. It has helped promote educational opportunities in Japan for students in Southeast Asia, while Japanese investment in the region has helped bolster the economies of both parties.

overseas development aid, compared with 11 percent each from the United States and Australia.[49] After the Asian economic crisis in 1997, Japan was the first industrial country to respond to the special financial needs of ASEAN countries.

Japanese leaders have supported exchange activities and study programs for ASEAN students. The Japan Scholarship Fund for ASEAN Youth was established in 1980, and provides US$1 million each year to enable students from ASEAN to study in many different fields in Japan—science, medicine, or economics, for example. Japan also started the Ship for Southeast Asia Youth program in 1973, and it continues to provide opportunities for ASEAN and Japanese youth to interact and develop friendships on a special ship. And, from 1984 to 2001, the ASEAN-Japan Youth Friendship Program has enabled 15,000 ASEAN youth to participate in study tours of Japan for several weeks.

In the last five years, Japan has made other major commitments to the ASEAN countries. Koh Tin Fook of Singapore's Ministry of Foreign Affairs commented on Japan's contribution to ASEAN:

> [Japan] has contributed substantial resources and expertise to help build up the region's infrastructure and human resource capacity in a wide range of fields ranging from economic development, environmental management, combating the spread of infectious diseases to disaster management.[50]

The partnership between ASEAN and Japan has been and remains the most important of all.

ASEAN LINKS WITH AUSTRALIA

Australia became the second dialogue partner with ASEAN in 1974. Northern parts of Australia are extremely close to Indonesia, the largest country in Southeast Asia. It is only 501 miles from Darwin in Australia's Northern Territory to West Timor in Indonesia. Half of the island of New Guinea (Irian Jaya) is part of Indonesia, and the other half is a former Australian territory (now independent Papua New Guinea, which has observer status in ASEAN).

Australia's assistance to ASEAN has focused on food and nutrition, trade and investment, science and technology, human resource development, water supply, eco-tourism, computers for the blind, and livestock help.[51] Australia entirely financed the first bridge across the Mekong River between Laos and Thailand, which opened in April 1994. The Mekong River, one of the world's longest at 2,870 miles (4,620 kilometers), originates in the mountains of Tibet and flows into the South China Sea (Eastern Sea) in the Mekong Delta in Vietnam, which was prominent during the Vietnam War.

Many ASEAN students choose to study in Australia. In 2005, 78,300 students from Indonesia, Malaysia, Singapore, and Thailand went to study in Australia.[52] Australia may be the only westernized country that teaches Southeast Asian languages in high school.

Australia has been one of East Timor's strongest supporters since 1999, when East Timor attempted to free itself of Indonesian rule. In fact, between 1999 and 2007, Australia has given over $570 million in assistance to East Timor.[53] In 2002, East Timor became the first new nation of the twenty-first century. Australia sent troops again in 2006 and 2007. Cooperation between Australia and ASEAN remains strong.

ASEAN RELATIONS WITH THE UNITED STATES

ASEAN, particularly Singapore, Malaysia, and Thailand, wants the United States to remain involved in the region to prevent domination by Japan or by an increasingly powerful China. The United States carries out joint military exercises with Singapore, Malaysia, Thailand, and the Philippines.

The United States has also closely cooperated with the ASEAN nations in efforts against terrorism. In October 2002, terrorists bombed a nightclub in a tourist resort on the island of Bali, Indonesia. Muslim extremists are also active in southern Thailand and in the southern Philippines. Indonesia (the country with the largest Muslim population in the world), Thailand, and the Philippines are eager to work with the United States to eliminate these threats.

With one of the world's largest and most dynamic economies, the United States represents an excellent market for ASEAN products. Asian supermarkets and grocery stores throughout the United States contain many ASEAN products. Many fruits from Thailand are now canned and exported to the United States for resale in Asian grocery stores. Long-grain jasmine Thai rice is commonly found in such stores. Red Bull, the popular high-energy drink, originates in Thailand.

However, ASEAN nations are sometimes troubled by what they see as United States interference in the region. In the wake of the 1997 economic crisis, Malaysia boldly rejected the policies of the International Monetary Fund, dominated by the United States, and went its own way. Thailand was deeply disappointed with U.S. failure to provide significant assistance at the time of the crisis. Thailand was also irritated by the United States' efforts to prevent a Thai, Dr. Supachai Panichpakdi, from becoming the director of the World Trade Organization, the important world body that makes the rules for global trade. The United States joined many other Western countries in supporting former prime minister of New Zealand Michael Moore, while most developing countries, particularly in Asia, supported Dr. Supachai. As a compromise, the WTO split the six-year term, with Moore taking the first three years, from 1999 to 2002, and Supachai the next three years.

The human rights problem in Burma/Myanmar is another stressful issue in the U.S.-ASEAN relationship. At the ASEAN Summit in November 2007, the United States indicated clearly that the situation in Myanmar would hold up any progress toward having an ASEAN-U.S. Free Trade Agreement.[55]

Despite such problems, the United States will remain an important partner of ASEAN. The dynamic, high technology sector of the United States is both an excellent market for ASEAN goods and a source of international investment. ASEAN feels more secure with a U.S. presence in the region to balance the power of Japan and China, although some argue that the United States has lost interest in the region because of its preoccupation with the oil-rich Middle East. Others disagree, emphasizing that the region is home to a huge Muslim population and that the Strait of Malacca between Singapore/ Peninsular Malaysia and the Indonesian island of Sumatra is a strategic "choke point," a key entry point to the Pacific Ocean that covers one third of the world's surface and is home to the economically dynamic Asia-Pacific region. The amount of world oil that passes through the strait is three times higher than that which passes through the Suez Canal.[56]

ASEAN LINKS WITH CHINA

ASEAN's partnership with China formed after many of the other partnerships, but with China's rise as a global and regional economic superpower it is becoming more important. The combined markets of China and ASEAN represent a gigantic 2 billion people (more than six times the size of the U.S. market). If China and ASEAN were to form a single free trade area, this would be the world's largest free trade area, far larger (in terms of population) than that of either the United States or the European Union. Nearly all the ASEAN nations have a large number of citizens with a Chinese cultural heritage and family ties to China, often dating back to colonial times. These individuals are frequently active in the business world.

In the year 2003 alone, ASEAN trade with China grew by 43 percent. A free trade area between ASEAN and China is to be fully implemented by 2010. In 2006, two-way trade between ASEAN and China had reached US$168.8 billion, up 23.4 percent from the previous year.[57] Trade with China now represents 8.5 percent of all of ASEAN's trade. Brunei, the Philippines, and Indonesia sold more to China than they bought (a trade surplus), while the other ASEAN countries bought more from China than they sold (a trade deficit). More ASEAN businesses are investing in China, and Chinese businesses are building more factories and offering more services in ASEAN countries. CP, Thailand's huge agribusiness company, has invested in every province of China, contributing to its growth in profits. CP is also in the process of negotiating a new joint venture with China to produce Chery brand Chinese cars in Thailand.

The economic developments among countries in Southeast Asia and China have increased dramatically, further encouraging civic and social projects between the region and China. A free trade zone between ASEAN and China would create the largest free trade area in the world. Here, a consumer buys clothes at the ASEAN-China Expo in Nanning, China in 2006.

China has a growing demand for the agricultural products and natural resources of Southeast Asia. Thailand and Vietnam are two of the world's three largest exporters of rice, and China will be an excellent market for Southeast Asian agricultural exports. China's booming, energy-hungry economy needs Southeast Asia's oil, found mainly in Indonesia, Malaysia, and Brunei. However, China also competes with ASEAN nations as an exporter of consumer goods such as textiles and electronics.

China is also important from a security perspective. China and ASEAN have established a dialogue and cooperated closely when ASEAN opposed Vietnamese intervention in Cambodia. Who controls the vast oil reserves in the South China Sea is both an economic and a security issue, since military, especially naval, power could be used to fight out any dispute over ownership.

China also has an intense interest in transportation and energy linkages with ASEAN. Among such areas of cooperation is the proposed Singapore-Kunming Rail Link. Kunming, the capital of Yunnan Province, is located directly above mainland Southeast Asia. If this railroad became a reality, visitors could easily travel from southern China to Myanmar, Laos, Thailand, and Malaysia, ending in Singapore at the tip of southern Malaysia. China is also helping to fund a highway network from Bangkok to Kunming.

ASEAN countries are deeply concerned that proposed dams on the part of the Mekong River in Chinese territory could reduce water flows to Southeast Asia. Tonle Sap, a huge freshwater lake in the center of Cambodia, is partially fed by the Mekong River. In an amazing process, the Mekong River reverses flow during the rainy season, greatly enlarging the lake, whose fish provide a major source of protein for Cambodians. Damming the river would harm both farming and fishing in Cambodia, Laos (the Mekong River runs through its center), and Vietnam, where the Mekong Delta is a major rice producer.

China has a sizeable and rapidly growing wealthy population.[58] China's inhabitants are potential consumers of Southeast Asian products, and Chinese tourism to ASEAN nations promises to accelerate in the years ahead. Planes flying into Bangkok are already often full of Chinese tour groups. In the long term, China and ASEAN, with a potentially economically integrated market of over 2 billion people, have the potential to be the world's largest market and a major economic force in the twenty-first century.

ASEAN LINKS WITH INDIA

Historical and cultural linkages between India and Southeast Asia go back thousands of years. Buddhism, a major religion of Southeast Asia's mainland countries, has its roots in India. The writing systems of Cambodia, Laos, Myanmar, and Thailand derive from Indian influences. Hinduism and Indian culture are strong influences on the Indonesian island of Bali. Many ASEAN countries, particularly Malaysia and Singapore, have substantial populations of Indians.

ASEAN-India dialogue is in its beginning stage. Though trade between the countries is not extensive, it has considerable potential for growth. Similar to China, India has a sizeable and rapidly growing wealthy population. Many have gained their wealth from India's growing computer software industry.[59] These individuals are now becoming tourists to ASEAN countries and potential consumers of ASEAN goods. If India, China, and ASEAN emerge as a free trade area, this will represent a market of approximately 3 billion people. At the November 2007 ASEAN Summit, India agreed to fast-track visas for ASEAN businessmen, and Indian Prime Minister Manmohan Singh set a trade target of US$50 billion with ASEAN by 2010.[60] An ASEAN-India free trade area is expected to be approved in July 2008.

ASEAN
Looks Ahead

In sum, our leaders see the ASEAN of the future as made up of societies that are open and caring, democratic and humane, pluralistic and participatory, blessed by social justice and the rule of law.[61]

—Rodolfo C. Severino, former
secretary-general, ASEAN

ASEAN HAS MADE GREAT CONTRIBUTIONS TO PEACE AND security in Southeast Asia. In its first two decades, from 1967 to 1987, it limited the influence of Communism. ASEAN united behind Thailand on the question of Vietnam's invasion of Cambodia, bringing it international recognition as an important and influential regional body.

ASEAN'S SUCCESSES

When Timor broke away from Indonesia in 1999–2000, chaos and violence threatened the area. In coordination with the United Nations, ASEAN directed regional peacekeeping forces to provide stability and peace. And when a coup occurred in Cambodia in 1997, with serious conflicts among Cambodian political groups, ASEAN sent a team that successfully negotiated an end to the fighting. ASEAN's role in resolving this conflict led the way for Cambodia to be admitted to ASEAN two years later, in 1999.

In its second two decades, from 1987 to 2007, ASEAN's major accomplishments included the creation of the ASEAN Free Trade Area (AFTA) and the acceleration of movement toward the ASEAN Economic Community by 2015. This has made the movement of goods and people across ASEAN borders much easier. ASEAN has reduced its level of dependence on richer nations outside the region, while Singapore, Thailand, Malaysia, and Indonesia have shown impressive productivity increases.[62]

In the 1990s, ASEAN expanded to include four new members—Vietnam (1995), Laos (1997), Myanmar (also 1997), and Cambodia (1999)—encompassing all the countries of the region within the organization. While Myanmar's inclusion has created some difficulties, membership may help its political and economic system to become more open.

ASEAN has been able to attract significant funding—the majority from Japan, Europe, Australia, New Zealand, the United States, and Canada—for regional projects and activities. As of 2003, Japan alone had contributed US$51.3 billion.[63] As China and India become more powerful economically, they also will be able to contribute further to ASEAN.

ASEAN'S WEAKNESSES

ASEAN's economic integration has proceeded slowly. The region's remarkable diversity in the economic, political, and cultural realms presents obstacles to economic integration. Having a common currency or one set of economic priorities and policies for all countries in the region is almost impossible. Political diversity prevents the region from having one set of rules about how businesses should operate. For example, in the Communist countries, potential investors must know how to handle complex bureaucracies. However, these can be overcome, as shown by Nike's success in Vietnam. With the huge economic differences between the ASEAN countries, it is important that the richer ASEAN countries provide assistance to the poorer ones. Thus far, the vast majority of assistance has come from outside the region.

People living in ASEAN countries still think of themselves as belonging to countries rather than the ASEAN region. As ASEAN addresses issues of people's health, poverty and inequality, the environment, and human rights, it may become easier for the population of the region to identify with the organization. Citizens of ASEAN nations generally know more about Europe or America than they do about each other. In a recent survey, only 37.5 percent of ordinary people responded that they could trust the other countries of the region to be good neighbors. Among high-ranking individuals surveyed, 59.8 percent stated that they could not trust all the countries of the region to be good neighbors.[64]

ASEAN also has a weak administrative structure, despite the strengthening of the ASEAN secretariat in 1992, because there is still no authority that can enforce compliance with regional policies. Thus, ASEAN remains an intergovernmental organization, with each country retaining control over its basic domestic policies. In addition, the budget system that calls for each ASEAN country, regardless of its wealth, to contribute the same amount must be reformed in order to be more equitable.

ASEAN continues to operate, as it has for 40 years, without a formal charter. ASEAN instead has operated with a loose, informal style called the "ASEAN Way." While this system has worked, it has resulted in a relatively weak secretariat. This contrasts with what happened in Europe, which in 1997 celebrated the fiftieth anniversary of the Treaty of Rome, the agreement that led to the European Union. An ASEAN charter is critically important to create a legal entity with real power that can force member states to follow agreements.[65]

Although the charter was formally approved on November 20, 2007, at the Thirteenth ASEAN Summit in Singapore (where they also celebrated the fortieth anniversary of ASEAN), it falls short in a number of areas. Though the charter calls for the establishment of an ASEAN human rights body, critics see the charter as weak because it lacks clear mechanisms for enforcing compliance in human rights or trade areas. The charter also fails to establish plans for a customs union, a procedure for all the countries to agree on the same tariffs or import taxes on goods coming from outside ASEAN.

Finally, because of the human rights' violations in Burma, Philippines President Gloria Macapagal Arroyo indicated that her country's congress may not ratify the charter, essentially vetoing it, since all ASEAN members must ratify the charter.[66] In January 2008, Singapore became the first ASEAN nation to ratify this historic document.

ASEAN'S FUTURE:
NEW LEADERSHIP AND RELATED CHALLENGES

ASEAN secretary-generals are elected on a rotating basis, every five years. The new secretary-general (as of January 2008), is Dr. Surin Pitsuwan, a Thai-Muslim and a Harvard Ph.D., from Thailand. Regarded as a dynamic leader, he is a former minister of foreign affairs.[67] His Muslim background will be particularly useful in working with the primarily Islamic ASEAN nations of Brunei, Indonesia, and Malaysia, and he has strong connections with Middle Eastern countries. He helped ASEAN solve the Timor crisis.

Opposing political ideologies aside, the leaders of ASEAN's member countries *(above)* are dedicated to the success of the region and the organization. They are committed to working together to ensure stability and prosperity on a collective and individual level.

If an ASEAN Union (similar to the European Union) and eventually an Asian Union can be achieved, then it is likely that the economic center of gravity of the world will shift to this region. The region's emphasis on education and human resource development may make it a dynamic leader of the twenty-first century. ASEAN will then be an integral part of an East Asian renaissance.[68] Its proximity to Japan, China, and India and its central location between Europe, the Middle East, China, Japan, and Australia gives it huge advantages. In the decades ahead, ASEAN will be at the center of the world's most dynamic economic region, a powerful engine of innovation and change.

CHRONOLOGY

1954   Southeast Asia Treaty Organization (SEATO) established.

1961   Association of Southeast Asia (ASA) established. ASA is the precursor to ASEAN.

1963   President Macapagal of the Philippines proposes the concept of MAPHILINDO (Malaysia, Philippines, Indonesia).

1963–1965   Confrontasi (conflict between Indonesia and its neighbors, the Philippines and Malaysia, over territorial claims).

1965   September 30 Gestapu (Gerakan 30 September) (September 30 Movement) Affair; failed communist coup in Indonesia dramatically affects the political future of Indonesia and Southeast Asia. Sukarno loses power. Emergence of Suharto and the New Order.

        President Johnson sends a huge contingent: 500,000 U.S. ground forces to Vietnam.

1966   In informal meetings with Indonesian and Malaysian colleagues, Thai Foreign Minister, Dr. Thanat Khoman, suggests the idea of establishing ASEAN.

1967   ASA terminated.

        Establishment of the Association of Southeast Asian Nations in Bangkok, Thailand. The ASEAN Declaration (also referred to as the Bangkok Declaration) is created.

1975   Cambodia (April 17), Laos (December 2), and Vietnam (April 30) become communist nations.

1977   SEATO terminated.

1978   Vietnam invades Cambodia and overthrows the Pol Pot regime, and then occupies the country for 10 years. Subsequently, ASEAN persuades the UN not to recognize the Vietnamese-imposed government as the legitimate ruler of Cambodia. Instead, following the recommendation of ASEAN, the UN recognizes a coalition of anti-Vietnamese Cambodian political groups, including the Khmer Rouge.

1984   Brunei obtains independence from the U.K. and joins ASEAN on January 8.

1992   Prime Minister Anand Panyarachun of Thailand proposes an ASEAN Free Trade Area (AFTA). AFTA is approved at the Fourth ASEAN Summit in Singapore.

1995   The Socialist Republic of Vietnam joins ASEAN.

1997   The Lao People's Democratic Republic and Union of Myanmar join ASEAN.

1999   The Kingdom of Cambodia joins ASEAN.

2003   ASEAN leaders decide to transform the region into an ASEAN Economic Community (AEC) by the year 2020. This is known as the Declaration of ASEAN Concord II or the Bali Concord II.

2006   Recommendation to create AEC by 2015, five years earlier than planned.

    UN General Assembly unanimously grants observer status to ASEAN.

2007   ASEAN Summit in Singapore and the celebration of the fortieth anniversary of ASEAN.

    ASEAN Charter approved.

2008   A Thai, Dr. Surin Pitsuwan takes over as secretary-general of ASEAN.

NOTES

Chapter 1

1. Kofi Annan, "'Unity in Diversity', Indonesia's Motto, Sums Up 'Our Common Humanity', says Secretary-General in Jakarta Address, Jakarta, Indonesia, February 16, 2000. Available online at *http://www.aseansec.org/6910.htm.*

2. Benajah Ticknor, *Journal of Voyages to Southeast Asia, South America & Duty Stations in United States as Surgeon* (1818–1852) Visual material: Projected image 3 reels.

3. Paul Brown, "Tsunami Cost Aceh a Generation and $4.4bn," *The Guardian*, January 22, 2005. Available online at *http://www.guardian.co.uk/tsunami/story/0,15671, 1396223,00.html.*

4. 2008 World Factbook. Available online at *https://www.cia.gov/library/publications/the-world-factbook/geos/sn.html.*

5. Denise Chong, *The Girl in the Picture: The Story of Kim Phuc, the Photograph, and the Vietnam War*. New York, NY: Viking, 2000.

Chapter 2

6. Jean Monnet, *Memoirs*. Garden City, NY: Doubleday, 1978.

7. Bernard K. Gordon, "Regionalism in Southeast Asia," *Man, State, and Society in Contemporary Southeast Asia*, ed. Robert O. Tilman. New York, NY: Praeger, 508.

8. Gordon, "Regionalism in Southeast Asia."

9. ASEAN Secretariat, "The Founding of ASEAN," op. cit.

10. Gerald W. Fry, Interview with Dr. Thanat Khoman, Bangkok, Thailand, April 24, 2007.

11. ASEAN Secretariat, "The Founding of ASEAN," op. cit.

12. Ibid.

13. Ibid.

Chapter 3

14. Shaun Narine, *Explaining ASEAN: Regionalism in Southeast Asia.* Boulder, Colo.: Lynne Rienner Publishers, 2002, 31–33.

15. Ronald D. Palmer and Thomas J. Reckford, "ASEAN Organizational Development—1970–1977," *Building ASEAN: 20 Years of Southeast Asian Cooperation.* New York, NY: Praeger, 1987, 39.

16. Michael Antolik, *ASEAN and the Diplomacy of Accommodation.* Armonk, NY: M.E. Sharpe, 1990, 8–10.

17. Gerald W. Fry, Interview with Dr. Suthad Setboonsarng, Bangkok, April 23, 2007. Dr. Suthad is a former Deputy Secretary-General of ASEAN.

18. Ibid.

Chapter 4

19. Prince Norodom Sihanouk and Wilfred G. Burchett, *My War with the CIA: The Memoirs of Prince Norodom Sihanouk.* New York, NY: Pantheon Books, 1973.

20. Stephen J. Morris, *Why Vietnam Invaded Cambodia: Political Culture and the Causes of War.* Stanford, Calif.: Stanford University Press, 1999.

21. Timothy Carney, *Kampuchea: Balance of Survival.* Bangkok: DD Books, 1981).

22. Narine, 45.

23. Narine, 47.

24. David Martin Jones and M.L.R. Smith, *ASEAN and East Asian International Relations: Regional Delusion.* Cheltenham, UK: Edward Elgar, 2006, 53–54.

25. Jones and Smith, 55.

Chapter 5

26. Amale Scally and Jayasinghe Wickramanayake, "An examination of the impact of AFTA on Southeast Asian foreign direct investment," *The Future of Foreign Investment in*

Southeast Asia, eds. Nick J. Freeman and Frank L. Bartels. New York, NY: RoutledgeCurzon, 2004, 49–79.

27. Scally and Wickramanayake, 53.

28. Kanokpan Lao-Araya, "How Can Cambodia, Lao PDR, Myanmar, and Viet Nam Cope with Revenue Lost Due to AFTA Tariff Reductions?" Manila: Asian Development Bank, 2002.

29. Indermit Gill and Homi Kharas, *An East Asian Renaissance: Ideas for Economic Growth.* Washington, D.C.: World Bank, 2007.

30. Nayan Chanda, *Bound Together: How Traders, Preachers, Adventurers, and Warriors Shaped Globalization.* New Haven, Conn.: Yale University Press, 2007.

Chapter 6

31. *2006 ASEAN-Japan Statistical Pocketbook.* Tokyo: ASEAN-Japan Centre, 2006, 96.

32. Christopher B. Roberts, "Trust elusive in regional community," *The Nation.* November 12, 2007.

33. Adrian Franklin, *Tourism: An Introduction.* London: SAGE Publications, 2003, 258.

34. David A. Feingold and Angelina Jolie, *Trading Women.* Watertown, Mass.: Documentary Educational Resources, 2003, VHS; see also Erik Cohen, *Thai Tourism: Hill Tribes, Islands and Open-ended Prostitution.* Bangkok: White Lotus, 1996.

35. CIA, *The 2008 World Factbook.* Available online at *https:// www.cia.gov/library/publications/the-world-factbook.*

36. Ibid.

37. Thomas D'Agnes, *From Condoms to Cabbages: An Authorized Biography of Mechai Viravaidya.* Bangkok: Post Books, 2001.

38. ASEAN Final Regional Seminar. "Framework of the ASEAN Work Programme on Industrial Relations,"

March 1, 2005. Available online at *http://www.aseansec. org/20916.pdf.*

39. Thomas Fuller, "No Blowing Smoke: Poppies Fade in Southeast Asia," *The New York Times Week in Review*, September 16, 2007. Available online at *http://www. nytimes.com/2007/09/16/weekinreview/16fuller.html?_ r=1&oref=slogin.*

40. Thomas Fuller, "Notorious Golden Triangle loses sway in the opium trade," *International Herald Tribune*, September 11, 2007. Available online at *http://www. iht. com/articles/2007/09/11/asia/golden.php.*

41. Keith Bradsher, "Governments Across Southeast Asia Work to Contain Bird Flu," *The New York Times*, January 26, 2004; Fred de Sam Lazaro, "Fatal Flu," *Online News-Hour*, April 7, 2005. Available online at *http://www.pbs. org/newshour/bb/health/jan-june05/flu_4-7.html.*

42. "ASEAN blueprint to fight bird flu," *The Times of India*, October 1, 2005. Available online at *http://timesofindia. indiatimes.com/articleshow/1249046.cms.*

43. Asian Development Bank, "Bird Flu." Available online at *http://www.adb.org/BirdFlu/default.asp.*

44. ASEAN, "Hanoi Plan of Action." Available online at *http://www.aseansec.org/8754.htm.*

45. Alexander C. Chandra, "ASEAN Foundation at Ten," *The Nation* (Bangkok), January 12, 2008, p. 8A.

Chapter 7

46. Rodolfo C. Severino, "ASEAN and the World," *Southeast Asia: In Search of an ASEAN Community*, 256–341. Singapore: Institute of Southeast Asian Studies, 2006, 332.

47. Robert M. Orr, *The Emergence of Japan's Foreign Aid Power*. New York, NY: Columbia University Press, 1990.

48. "Japan looks to deepen ASEAN ties," *Bangkok Post*, June 7, 2007. Available online at *http://bangkokpost.com.*

49. *2006 ASEAN-Japan Statistical Pocketbook*, 30.

50. "Japan looks to deepen ASEAN ties." op. cit.

51. Severino, 311.

52. Nitya Pibulsonggram, address at the ASEAN Post Ministerial Conference + 1 Session with Australia. Available online at *http://www.boi.go.th/english/how/speeches_detail.asp?id=291*.

53. Australian Government, Australia's Aid Program. "Overseas Aid—East Timor." Available online at *http://www.ausaid.gov.au/country/country.cfm?CountryId=911*.

54. "US-ASEAN ties off again, on again." *The Nation* (Bangkok), September 27, 2007. Available online at *http://www.nationmultimedia.com/search/page.news.php?clid=11&id=30050392*.

55. Susan C. Schwab, Media Roundtable–U.S. Embassy Singapore, November 19, 2007. Available online at *http://www.ustr.gov/assets/Document_Library/Transcripts/2007/November/asset_upload_file881_13619.pdf*.

56. "US-ASEAN ties off again, on again." op.cit.

57. Umesh Pandey, "Cautious Integration," *Bangkok Post*, June 9, 2007. Available online at *http://bangkokpost.com/*.

58. Davies, James B. et al. "The World Distribution of Household Wealth." Helsinki: UNU-WIDER, December 2006.

59. Ibid.

60. "India fast-tracks visas for ASEAN businessmen," *Bangkok Post*, December 18, 2007. Available online at *http://bangkokpost.com/*; see also Shri Prakash, Vanita Roy, and Sanjay Ambedkar eds., *India and ASEAN: Economic Partnership in the 1990s and Future Prospects*. New Delhi: Gyan Publishing House, 1996.

Chapter 8

61. Rodolfo Severino, "ASEAN Rises to the Challenge." Jakarta: The ASEAN Secretariat, 1999, 9.

62. Michael Sarel, "Growth and Productivity in ASEAN Countries." Washington, D.C.: IMF, 1997, Working Paper No. 97/97.

63. Takaaki Kojima, *Japan and ASEAN: Partnership for a Stable and Prosperous Future.* Singapore: Institute of Southeast Asian Studies [ISEAS], 2006, 6.

64. Christopher B. Roberts, op. cit.

65. Rodolfo C. Severino, ed., *Framing the ASEAN Charter: An ISEAS Perspective.* Singapore: ISEAS, 2005, 7; see also Termsak Chalermpalanupap, "In Defense of the ASEAN Charter," *The Nation* (Bangkok), January 15, 2008, p.9A.

66. Wayne Arnold, "Historic ASEAN charter reveals divisions," *International Herald Tribune*, November 20, 2007. Available online at *http://www.iht.com/*.

67. Surin Pitsuwan, "Future Directions for ASEAN," in *The 2nd ASEAN Reader*, eds. Sharon Siddiqe and Sree Kumar, 486–488. Singapore: ISEAS, 2003; see also "Surin: ASEAN Integration 'Difficult.'" *Bangkok Post*, May 18, 2007. Available online at *http://bangkokpost.com/*.

68. Gill, et al., op.cit.

BIBLIOGRAPHY

"Ailing Proton Looks to Mecca." *Asia Sentinel*, November 22, 2007. Available online. URL: http://www.asiasentinel.com.

"Angkor Wat facing a 500-year-old problem." *Taipei Times*, March 26, 2007. Available online. URL: http://www.taipei times.com/News/world/archives/2007/03/26/2003353917.

Annan, Kofi. "'Unity in Diversity', Indonesia's motto, sums up 'our common humanity', says secretary-general in Jakarta address." Jakarta, Indonesia, February 16, 2000. Available online. URL: http://www.aseansec.org/6910.htm.

Antolik, Michael. *ASEAN and the Diplomacy of Accommodation*. Armonk, NY: M.E. Sharpe, 1990.

Arnold, Wayne. "Historic ASEAN charter reveals division." *International Herald Tribune*, November 20, 2007. Available online. URL: http://www.iht.com/.

ASEAN Secretariat. "The Founding of ASEAN." Jakarta: ASEAN Secretariat, 2007. Available online. URL: http://www.aseansec.org/7071.htm.

ASEAN: The First Twenty Years. Singapore: Federal Publications (for the ASEAN Secretariat), 1987.

Bradsher, Keith. "Governments Across Southeast Asia Work to Contain Bird Flu." *The New York Times*, January 26, 2004.

Brown, Paul. "Tsunami cost Aceh a generation and $4.4bn." *The Guardian*, January 22, 2005. Available online. URL: http://www.guardian.co.uk/world/2005/jan/22/tsunami2004.inter nationalaidanddevelopment.

Carney, Timothy Michael. *Kampuchea: Balance of Survival*. Bangkok: DD Books, 1983.

Chanda, Nayan. *Bound Together: How Traders, Preachers, Adventurers, and Warriors Shaped Globalization*. New Haven, Conn.: Yale University Press, 2007.

Chong, Denise. *The Girl in the Picture: The Story of Kim Phuc, the Photograph, and the Vietnam War.* New York, NY: Viking, 2000.

Crone, Donald K. *The ASEAN States: Coping with Dependence.* New York, NY: Praeger, 1983.

Curry, Andrew. "Angkor Was a Vast City." *Discover* magazine: The Year in Science 2007, January 15, 2008.

D'Agnes, Thomas. *From Condoms to Cabbages: An Authorized Biography of Mechai Viravaidya.* Bangkok: Post Books, 2001.

de Sam Lazaro, Fred. "Fatal Flu." Online NewsHour April 7, 2005. Available online. URL: http://www.pbs.org/newshour/bb/health/jan-june05/flu_4-7.html.

Emmerson, Donald K., ed. *Hard Choices: Security, Democracy, and Regionalism in Southeast Asia.* Stanford, Calif.: Walter H. Shorenstein Asia-Pacific Research Center, 2008.

Fuller, Thomas. "Notorious Golden Triangle loses sway in the opium trade." *International Herald Tribune*, September 11, 2007. Available online. URL: http://www.iht.com/articles/2007/09/11/asia/golden.php.

Gabilaia, Tamar. "Malaysian Proton and AFTA: threat or advantage?" *TED Case Studies*, June 2001. Available online. URL: http://www.american.edu/TED/proton.htm.

Gill, Indermit and Homi Kharas. *An East Asian Renaissance: Ideas for Economic Growth.* Washington, D.C.: World Bank, 2007.

Gordon, Bernard K. "Regionalism in Southeast Asia." *Man, State, and Society in Contemporary Southeast Asia*, edited by Robert O. Tilman. New York, NY: Praeger, 1969, 506–522.

Heong, Chee Yoke. "Malaysia's Proton struggles on." *Asia Times*, August 26, 2003. Available online. URL: http:www.atimes.com.

"India fast-tracks visas for ASEAN businessmen." *Bangkok Post*, December 18, 2007. Available online. URL: http://bangkok post.com/.

"Japan looks to deepen ASEAN ties." *Bangkok Post*, June 7, 2007. Available online. URL: http://bangkokpost.com.

Jones, David Martin and M.L.R. Smith. *ASEAN and East Asian International Relations: Regional Delusion.* Cheltenham, UK: Edward Elgar, 2006.

Kojima, Takaaki. *Japan and ASEAN: Partnership for a Stable and Prosperous Future.* Singapore: ISEAS, 2006.

Lao-Araya, Kanokpan. "How Can Cambodia, Lao PDR, Myanmar, and Viet Nam Cope with Revenue Lost Due to AFTA Tariff Reductions?" Manila: Asian Development Bank, 2002.

Monnet, Jean. *Memoirs.* Garden City, NY: Doubleday, 1978.

Morris, Stephen J. *Why Vietnam Invaded Cambodia: Political Culture and the Causes of War.* Calif.: Stanford University Press, 1999.

Narine, Shaun. *Explaining ASEAN: Regionalism in Southeast Asia.* Boulder, Colo.: Lynne Rienner Publishers, 2002.

Naya, Seiji and Pearl Imada. *AFTA: The Way Ahead.* Singapore: ISEAS, 1993.

Nevins, Joseph and Nancy Lee Peluso. *Taking Southeast Asia to Market: Commodities, Nature, and People in the Neoliberal Age.* Ithaca, NY: Cornell University Press, 2008.

Orr, Robert M. *The Emergence of Japan's Foreign Aid Power.* New York, NY: Columbia University Press, 1990.

Orwell, George. *Burmese Days.* New York, NY: Harcourt, 1962.

Palmer, Ronald D. and Thomas J. Reckford. "ASEAN Organizational Development—1970–1977." *Building ASEAN: 20 Years of Southeast Asian Cooperation*. New York, NY: Praeger, 1987, 37–57.

Pandey, Umesh. "Cautious Integration." *Bangkok Post*, June 9, 2007. Available online. URL: http://bangkokpost.com/

Pitsuwan, Surin. "Future Directions for ASEAN." *The 2nd ASEAN Reader*, edited by Sharon Siddique and Sree Kumar. Singapore: ISEAS, 2003, 486–488.

Roberts, Christopher B. "Trust elusive in regional community." *The Nation*, November 12, 2007. Available online. URL: http://www.nationmultimedia.com/.

Sarel, Michael. "Growth and Productivity in ASEAN Countries." Washington, D.C.: IMF, 1997, Working Paper No. 97/97.

Scally, Amale and Jayasinghe Wickramanayake. "An examination of the impact of AFTA on Southeast Asian foreign direct investment." *The Future of Foreign Investment in Southeast Asia*, edited by Nick J. Freeman and Frank L. Bartels. New York, NY: RoutledgeCurzon, 2004, 49–79.

Severino, Rodolfo C. "ASEAN and the World." *Southeast Asia: In Search of an ASEAN Community*. Singapore: ISEAS, 2006, 256–341.

———. "ASEAN Rises to the Challenge." Jakarta: The ASEAN Secretariat, 1999.

———., ed. *Framing the ASEAN Charter*. Singapore: ISEAS, 2005.

"Surin: ASEAN Integration 'Difficult.'" *Bangkok Post*, May 18, 2007. Available online. URL: http://bangkokpost.com/.

Suryadinata, Leo. "Towards an ASEAN Charter: Promoting an ASEAN Regional Identity." *Framing the ASEAN Charter*, edited by Rodolfo C. Severino. Singapore: ISEAS, 2005, 41–44.

Teh, Robert R., Raymond Yee, and Noordin Azhari, eds. *AFTA Reader: The Sixth ASEAN Summit and the Acceleration of AFTA*. Jakarta: ASEAN Secretariat, 1998, volume 5.

Ticknor, Benajah. *Journal of Voyages to Southeast Asia, South America & Duty Stations in United States as Surgeon* (1818–1852).

2006 ASEAN-Japan Statistical Pocketbook. Tokyo: ASEAN-Japan Centre, 2006.

Wong, John, Zou Keyuan, and Zeng Huaqun, eds. *China-ASEAN Relations: Economic and Legal Dimensions*. Singapore: World Scientific Publishing, 2006.

Wunderlich, Jens-Uwe. *Regionalism, Globalisation and International Order: Europe and Southeast Asia*. Burlington, Vt.: Ashgate, 2007.

Yang, Dao. *Hmong at the Turning Point*. Minneapolis: World-Bridge Associates, 1993.

WEB SITES

The ASEAN Foundation
http://www.aseanfoundation.org/.

ASEAN-Japan Centre
http://www.asean.or.jp/.

ASEAN News Network
http://www.aseannewsnetwork.com.

ASEAN Science and Technology Network (ASTNET)
http://www.astnet.org/.

The Asia Europe Meeting (ASEM)
http://ec.europa.eu/external_relations/asem/intro/index.htm.

Twelfth ASEAN Summit:
  "One Caring and Sharing Community"
  http://www.gov.ph/files/Primerfinal.doc.

U.S.-ASEAN Business Council
  http://www.us-asean.org/.

FURTHER READING

Alberti, Theresa and Blanks, Natascha Alex. *Vietnam ABCs: A Book About the People and Places of Vietnam*. Minneapolis, Minn.: Picture Window Books, 2007.

Burr, Rachel. *Vietnam's Children in a Changing World*. New Brunswick, NJ: Rutgers University Press, 2006.

Caputo, Philip. *10,000 Days of Thunder: A History of the Vietnam War*. New York, NY: Atheneum Books for Young Readers, 2005.

Chandler, David P. *The Land and People of Cambodia*. New York, NY: HarperCollins, 1991.

Church, Peter, ed. *A Short History of South-East Asia*. Singapore, 4th ed. (Asia): John Wiley & Sons, 2005.

Doeden, Matt. *Laos in Pictures*. Minneapolis, Minn.: Twenty-First Century Books, 2007.

Flores, Jamil Maiden and Jun Abad. *ASEAN at 30*. Jakarta: Association of Southeast Asian Nations, 1997 (Also available as a video).

Houle, Michelle. *The Vietnamese*. Detroit, Mich.: Greenhaven Press, 2005.

Kras, Sara Louise. *Cambodia: Enchantment of the World*. New York, NY: Children's Press, 2005.

Kummer, Patricia. *Singapore: Enchantment of the World*. New York, NY: Children's Press, 2003.

Larkin, Emma. *Finding George Orwell in Burma*. New York, NY: Penguin Books, 2005.

Miller, Debra A. *Indonesia*. Farmington Hills, Mich.: Lucent Books, 2005.

Mirpuri, Gouri and Robert Cooper. *Indonesia*. Tarrytown, NY: Benchmark Books, 2001.

Munan, Heidi and Foo Yuk Yee. *Malaysia*. Tarrytown, NY: Benchmark Books, 2002.

Oleksy, Walter. *The Philippines: Enchantment of the World*. New York, NY: Children's Press, 2000.

Phillips, Douglas A. *Southeast Asia*. New York, NY: Chelsea House, 2006.

Rau, Dana Meachen. *Thailand*. Tarrytown, NY: Benchmark Books, 2007.

Saffron, Walden. *ASEAN: The Next 30 Years*. Essex, United Kingdom: The World of Information, 1998.

Sandhu, K.S. et al., eds. *The ASEAN Reader*. Singapore: ISEAS, 1992.

Severino, Rodolfo C. *Southeast Asia in Search of an ASEAN Community: Insights from the Former ASEAN Secretary-General*. Singapore: ISEAS, 2006.

Sullivan, James. *Over the Moat: Love Among the Ruins of Imperial Vietnam*. New York, NY: Picador, 2004.

Tarling, Nicholas. *Regionalism in Southeast Asia*. New York, NY: Routledge, 2006.

Tope, Lily Rose R. and Detch P. Nonan-Mercado. *Philippines*. Tarrytown, NY: Benchmark Books, 2002.

Trocki, Carl A. *Singapore: Wealth, Power, and the Culture of Control*. New York, NY: Routledge, 2006.

Vang, Chia Youyee. *Hmong in Minnesota*. St. Paul, Minn.: Minnesota Historical Society Press, 2008.

Weatherbee, Donald E. *Historical Dictionary of United States–Southeast Asia Relations*. Lanham, Md.: Scarecrow Press, 2008.

Willis, Terri. *Vietnam*. New York, NY: Children's Press, 2002.

Yin, Saw Myat. *Myanmar*. Tarrytown, NY: Benchmark Books, 2001.

WEB SITES

Official ASEAN Web site
  http://www.aseansec.org/.

ASEAN tourism with the theme of
  "ASEAN: Asia's Perfect 10 Paradise."
  http://www.asean-tourism.com.

ASEAN University Network (AUN).
  http://www.aun-sec.org/.

ASEANWeb, the major Web site
  with information on ASEAN.
  http://www.aseansec.org/9156.htm.

PICTURE CREDITS

PAGE

INDEX

ABOUT THE CONTRIBUTORS

Author **GERALD W. FRY** is a professor of international/intercultural Education at the University of Minnesota. For over five decades, he has worked professionally in Southeast Asia in diverse capacities. Fry holds a B.A. in economics from Stanford, a M.P.A. in Public and International Affairs from Princeton, and a Ph.D. in international development education from Stanford. He has published many books and articles. From 2006–2007 he was a Visiting Research Scholar at Nagoya University in Japan.

Series editor **PEGGY KAHN** is a professor of political science at the University of Michigan–Flint. She teaches world and European politics. She has been a social studies volunteer in the Ann Arbor, Michigan, public schools, and she helps prepare college students to become teachers. She has a Ph.D. in political science from the University of California, Berkeley and a B.A. in history and government from Oberlin College.